HOW GOD USED R. A. TORREY

HOW GOD USED R. A. TORREY

A SHORT BIOGRAPHY AS TOLD THROUGH HIS SERMONS

FRED SANDERS

MOODY PUBLISHERS
CHICAGO

All Scripture quotations, unless otherwise indicated, are taken from the King James Version.

Scripture quotations marked RV are from the Revised Version of the Bible.

Edited by James Vincent
Interior design: Ragont Design
Cover design: Erik M. Peterson
Cover photo of R. A. Torrey courtesy of Moody Bible Institute archives; October 2014.

Library of Congress Cataloging-in-Publication Data

Sanders, Fred (Fred R.)
How God used R. A. Torrey : a short biography as told through his sermons / Fred Sanders.
pages cm
Includes bibliographical references.
ISBN 978-0-8024-1268-3 (paperback)
1. Torrey, R. A. (Reuben Archer), 1856–1928. 2. Evangelists—United States—Biography. 3. Catholic Church—Sermons. 4. Sermons, American. I. Torrey, R. A. (Reuben Archer), 1856–1928. Sermons Selections. II. Title.
BV3785.T6S36 2015
269'.2092—dc23
[B]

2015001013

We hope you enjoy this book from Moody Publishers. Our goal is to provide high-quality, thought-provoking books and products that connect truth to your real needs and challenges. For more information on other books and products written and produced from a biblical perspective, go to www.moodypublishers.com or write to:

Moody Publishers
820 N. LaSalle Boulevard
Chicago, IL 60610

1 3 5 7 9 10 8 6 4 2

Printed in the United States of America

Contents

INTRODUCTION

Torrey and His Sermons

Reuben Archer Torrey, known better as R. A. Torrey (1856–1928), was one of the most influential preachers in modern church history. During the first two decades of the twentieth century, he was widely acknowledged as the most important evangelist, having inherited the mantle of Dwight L. Moody and traveled the world with the gospel message.

His accomplishments were impressive: he was Moody's right-hand man during the great Chicago World's Fair evangelism campaign, pastor of Moody Church, superintendent of Moody Bible Institute, and then MBI president from 1899–1904.[1] Later he would become the first academic dean of the Bible Institute of Los Angeles, or BIOLA (today Biola University), founding pastor of the Church of the Open Door in Los Angeles, and final editor of *The Fundamentals*. A large plaque honoring him at Biola University features a bust of his likeness over the words:

AUTHOR * PREACHER * TEACHER
EVANGELIST TO FOUR CONTINENTS

and adds, "He Being Dead Yet Speaketh" (Hebrews 11:4).

Torrey's words are still powerful today, and this book offers an opportunity to hear his witness afresh in our own time. It reprints thirteen of his sermons, and publishes, for the first time anywhere, a brief autobiographical sketch that he wrote (see the appendix).

The sermons are selected from the three major productive periods of his ministry: the years when he served as one of Dwight Moody's most trusted workers (1889–1904), his great round-the-world preaching tours (1902–1911), and his time of ministry at the Bible Institute of Los Angeles (1912–1924). But by the time he began collaborating with Moody, Torrey had already gathered the education, experience, and formation that he would need in order to be so useful in ministry. What made him uniquely powerful throughout his life was his combination of academic prestige, ability as a teacher, and evangelistic fervor. Here is how he became who he was.

Education and Formation

Torrey was from a wealthy family, and graduated from a private high school in New York at age fourteen. He had to wait another year to be eligible for college, and then he enrolled at Yale. As an adult, Torrey would look back on his time in college as mostly misspent on partying and triviality: card-playing, dancing, and drinking to excess. His family was Christian, and Torrey's mother wanted him to be a minister, but Torrey had his mind on becoming a lawyer. In high school, Torrey contemplated what it would mean to become a professing Christian and a member of the church. He believed everything a broad-minded citizen of the nineteenth century needed to believe about Christian doctrine, with only a handful of skeptical reservations about some of the harder doctrines. He was willing to identify himself publicly with the church. But as he read the church membership requirements closely, he recognized that to be Christian meant to surrender your will and your future plans to the lordship of Jesus Christ. That was something he was not willing to do. After all, he wanted to be a lawyer, but Christ might want him to do something else. Perhaps he would even have to become a preacher, and, as he noted in a later autobiographical sketch, "then life would not be worth living." Unwilling to surrender his sovereignty and self-possession, Torrey set aside the question of becoming a member of the Christian church.

But Torrey had faced the claims of Christ, and rejecting them took a toll on him. He apparently was well aware that he had confronted someone who was rightfully his Lord, and had opted to avoid settling his accounts with that person. In his junior year at Yale, Torrey was wracked with guilt over his rejection of Christ's rightful claims. One night it all pressed in on him at once, and he actually attempted suicide. Unable to find the razor with which he planned to kill himself, he instead fell to his knees and surrendered to Christ.

This act of absolute surrender was not just a momentary crisis in a young college student's life with no effects. Though it took time for him to work out the implications, it was the turning point in the course of his life. Torrey had dug himself into an intellectual hole in the years he had been on the run spiritually. After his conversion his doctrinal views continued to be liberal on many fronts: he was weak on confessing the full deity of Christ, and he rejected eternal punishment and the inerrancy of Scripture for several more years. But now that he had crossed over the watershed, it was inevitable that all those doctrines and more would fall into place. If liberalism is the refusal to accept hard doctrines, the remnants of Torrey's liberalism were doomed to fade away, because he had already, in principle, decided to accept whatever God had revealed in Scripture.

What marked his life from that point on was the absolute surrender to Jesus. He would emphasize it later in his personal evangelism strategy, which sometimes included accusing the self-sufficient and self-righteous of having committed "treason against the high king of heaven." He would also underline it in his teaching on the baptism of the Holy Spirit, which focused on surrendering your will to God and consecrating your life to service. And writing in the 1920s, he would name as the number one reason "Why God Used D. L. Moody" that his mentor Moody was "a fully surrendered man." Whatever developments lay ahead for Torrey, the shape of his Christian life was set on that night of which he said: "I dropped on my knees beside the open drawer and promised God that if He would take the awful burden off my heart, I would preach the Gospel."

After graduating from Yale, Torrey completed graduate studies at Yale Divinity School, obtained a second degree, and was licensed for ministry in the Congregational church. In 1878, Dwight Moody came through New Haven on a preaching tour, and several students from the divinity school went to hear him. Though many of the students were smugly convinced of their superiority over the undereducated Moody, Torrey found his message compelling, and even worked as a volunteer minister in the inquiry room.

Both of Torrey's parents died when he was twenty-one years old, just as he was launching into his career as a pastor in Ohio and then in Minneapolis. In one of his early pastorates, Torrey met and married Clara Belle Smith. Very early in his ministry, Torrey read Charles Finney's *Lectures on Revival* and became convinced that the local church ought to be run in such a way that revival was its ordinary condition. The main practical result of this philosophy was that he trained each member of the congregation in personal evangelism.

In 1882, with his wife and their first child, Torrey resigned his pastorate in order to devote two years to graduate studies in Germany. German universities enjoyed the reputation of being the most rigorous and critical in the theological world at that time, and Torrey must have been eager to test his Yale theological education against the best that Germany could offer. From among his options, Torrey chose very conservative German theological programs to study at (the University of Leipzig and the University of Erlangen), and he worked hard in a range of subjects from Old Testament through apologetics and doctrine. He kept a diary during this time abroad, recording the impressions the lectures and discussions made on him. He must have made many doctrinal decisions while doing this advanced work in the theological disciplines, but at some point he apparently decided that he had learned as much as he needed to for his future work. (Financial limitations and second pregnancy also contributed to cutting the two-year plan short.) The year of study in Germany seems to have confirmed him in the plans he had already made for his life. When Torrey returned from Germany, he no longer had any hint of indecisiveness about investing his life in the work of a pastor.

Testing in Early Ministry

Returning to America, Torrey threw himself into his ministry in the new Open Door Church in Minneapolis, and later at the People's Church, also in Minneapolis. For the next several years, Torrey made a number of moves that showed how serious, even radical, his vision of the urban pastorate of the late nineteenth century was. He and his family embraced for some time a life of total dependence on God for financial support, following the model of George Mueller's "Life of Faith," according to which he did not make his needs known to anyone but God. He became convinced that sprinkling was an unbiblical mode of receiving water baptism, and Clara and he were baptized by immersion. He experienced divine physical healing personally, and prayed for a number of people, who were also healed by God.

In his pastorates after his return from Germany, Torrey became increasingly committed to preaching social reform, especially temperance. (He and Clara had taken a temperance pledge many years before.) For a while, Torrey accepted numerous invitations to lead a variety of civic organizations, and cooperated with numerous other churches. In time his schedule became too busy, utterly dominated by these meetings, all of them good in themselves. Each of them was an expression of his philosophy that denominational differences should be strictly subordinated to a unified effort of all Christian churches in any given city to glorify God and help the community thrive. But gradually, multiple commitments to these good causes were proving too much for him. In later years he would recall James Stalker's warning that "As soon as the devil sees a young minister likely to be of use in the kingdom of God he gets on his back and rides him to death with engagements."

He resolved that he would focus on the one thing he knew God had called him to do, which was to preach the gospel. In a single afternoon he wrote seven resignation letters to seven different organizations. His ministry was taking on the form and the focus that it would retain for the rest of his life.

In his years of ministry R. A. Torrey wrote dozens of books, as well as thousands of pages of Bible study helps, editorials, and columns for magazines like *The King's Business*. His total output in these fields was massive, and all of them are useful in coming to understand his life and ministry. But it is his sermons that give the best sense of what he was all about. Torrey was a preacher first and last, which is why this book presents his life and thought through reprinting sermons chosen from the three major periods of his ministry.

In reproducing these thirteen sermons, I have retained the style found in the original books. However, where unusual capitalization, spelling, or punctuation appeared, I have changed sentences to conform with modern style and usage.

Note

1. Torrey continued to be called superintendent of the Chicago Bible Institute through 1904, but in effect he served as president of the institute after Moody's death (soon renamed Moody Bible Institute); the school now recognizes

Torrey's presidency as spanning 1899–1904. Beginning in 1902 Torrey was superintendent/president in absentia most of the time due to his international preaching tours. In 1904 James M. Gray accepted the position of academic dean, but in effect served as the third president of the institute. See James M. Vincent, *The MBI Story* (Chicago: Moody, 2011), 41, 44.

PART 1

THE YEARS WITH MOODY

INTRODUCTION

Real Salvation and Wholehearted Service

R. A. Torrey's competence in ministry eventually came to the notice of Dwight L. Moody (1837–1899), who was in need of somebody with the academic credentials to run his new Chicago Bible institute. From his first encounter with Moody at Yale Divinity School, Torrey had recognized this uneducated former shoe salesman—now a visionary evangelist and Bible educator—as a man who knew what mattered. When Moody called, Torrey answered immediately, and radically subordinated his own ministry to the needs of Dwight Moody for as long as Moody needed him.

Torrey drafted a curriculum for the Bible institute and along with Moody oversaw the massive evangelistic work connected with the 1893 World's Fair in Chicago, while continuing to pastor and chair several nondenominational organizations whose work was vital to evangelism. In his work as Moody's associate, Torrey devised new ways of training large numbers of laypeople in Bible knowledge and personal evangelism.

During those years Torrey honed his trademark personal evangelism methods. Torrey's approach was certainly direct, even confrontational. Torrey had pondered the deep mysteries of Christianity, grappled with the whole Bible, led many people to Christ, and seen the work of God in the lives of numerous church members. Cognizant of all these things, Torrey believed that a Christian should engage directly with people he meets, quickly discern their spiritual needs, and bring the ideas and the very words of Scripture to their attention in a definite way. In the many training books he wrote about how to evangelize, Torrey was always careful to emphasize the need for guidance from the Holy Spirit in discerning the needs of people one meets. But what most strikes the reader who picks up these books today is the prompt, definite, and confident way Torrey could perceive a person's spiritual condition. All the relevant words of Scripture, all the relevant arguments, all the helpful appeals would snap into place as soon as Torrey had made a judgment about who he was dealing with.

When D. L. Moody died in 1899, many Christian leaders felt that a great age of the church had passed away with him. R. A. Torrey, who had as good a claim to being Moody's second-in-command as anybody, had a different view of the matter. Torrey began preaching that the death of Moody was not a sign that great things were past, but that greater things were coming. Just as the death of Moses was a call for the generation of Joshua to move on to the land of promise, Torrey viewed the death of Moody as a call for the next generation to seek even greater things from God. Along with preaching this message, Torrey began organizing prayer groups to ask God to awaken the church and save the lost.

1

Ten Reasons Why I Believe The Bible Is the Word of God

AT THE PODIUM

This early sermon on the authority of Scripture provides a glimpse of Torrey's mental and spiritual development. As a young minister, he had been slow to accept the full inspiration of Scripture, and he begins this sermon with a partial testimony to how his mind changed. One of the secrets of Torrey's effectiveness in preaching was that he mixed apologetics and direct evangelistic appeal judiciously, confronting his audience with convincing arguments and direct invitations to respond to the gospel. This sermon is an early example of that method, a sermon Torrey gave often in various forms. In fact, at the other end of his career, in the 1920s, Torrey would deliver a version of this sermon on the radio and also have it recorded: the only audio recording we have of R. A. Torrey preaching.[1]

SOURCE: R. A. Torrey. "Ten Reasons Why I Believe the Bible Is the Word of God." Charles Leach. *Our Bible: How We Got It.* Chicago: Moody Press, 1898, 114–32.

I was brought up to believe that the Bible was the Word of God. In early life I accepted it as such upon the authority of my parents and never gave the question any serious thought. But later in life my faith in the Bible was utterly shattered through the influence of the writings of a very celebrated, scholarly, and brilliant skeptic. I found myself face-to-face with the question, *Why* do you believe the Bible is the Word of God?

I had no satisfactory answer. I determined to go to the bottom of this question. If satisfactory proof could not be found that the Bible was God's Word, I would give the whole thing up, cost what it might. If satisfactory proof could be found that the Bible was God's Word, I would take my stand upon it, cost what it might. I doubtless had many friends who could have answered the question satisfactorily, but I was unwilling to confide to them the struggle that was going on in my own heart; so I sought help from God and from books, and after much painful study and thought came out of the darkness of skepticism into the broad daylight of faith and certainty that the Bible from beginning to end is God's Word. The following pages are largely the outcome of that experience of conflict and final victory. I will give ten reasons why I believe the Bible is the Word of God.

Ten Reasons the Bible Is the Word of God: 1. The Testimony of Jesus Christ

First, *on the ground of the testimony of Jesus Christ.*

Many people accept the authority of Christ who do not accept that of the Bible as a whole. We all must accept His authority. He is accredited to us by five divine testimonies: by the testimony of the divine life He lived; by the testimony of the divine words He spoke; by the testimony of the divine works He wrought; by the divine attestation of the resurrection from the dead; and by the testimony of His divine influence upon the history of mankind. But if we accept the authority of Christ we must accept the authority of the Bible as a whole. He testifies definitely and specifically to the divine authorship of the whole Bible.

We find His testimony as to the Old Testament in Mark 7:13. Here He calls the law of Moses the "Word of God." That, of course, covers only the first five books of the Old Testament, but in Luke 24:27 we read, "And beginning at Moses and all the prophets, he expounded unto them in *all the scriptures* the things concerning himself" (emphasis added), and in the forty-fourth verse He said, "All things must be fulfilled, which were written in the law of Moses, and in the prophets, and in the psalms." The Jews divided the Old Testament into three parts—the Law, the Prophets, and the Psalms—and Christ takes up each of these parts and sets the stamp of His authority upon it. In John 10:35 Christ says, "The scripture cannot be broken," thereby teaching the absolute accuracy and inviolability of the Old Testament. More specifically still, if possible, in Matthew 5:18, Jesus says, "One jot or one tittle shall in no wise pass from the law, till all be fulfilled." A jot is the smallest letter in the Hebrew alphabet—less than half the size of any other letter, and a tittle is the merest point of a consonant—less than the cross we put on a "t"—and Christ here declares that the Scripture is absolutely true, down to the smallest letter or point of a letter. So if we accept the authority of Christ, we must accept the divine authority of the entire Old Testament.

Now, as to the New Testament, we find Christ's endorsement of it in John 14:26: "The Holy Ghost, whom the Father will send in my name, he shall teach you all things, and bring all things to your remembrance, whatsoever I have said unto you." Here we see that not only was the teaching of the apostles to be fully inspired, but also their recollection of what Christ Himself taught. We are sometimes asked how we know that the apostles correctly reported what Jesus said—"may they not have forgotten?" True, they might forget, but Christ Himself tells us that in the Gospels we have, not the apostles' recollection of what He said but the Holy Ghost's recollection, and the Spirit of God never forgets. In John 16:13–14, Christ said that the Holy Ghost should guide the apostles into "all truth," therefore in the New Testament teaching we have the whole sphere of God's truth. The teaching of the apostles is more complete than that of Jesus Himself, for He says in John 16:12, "I have yet many things to say unto you, but ye cannot bear them now. Howbeit, when he, the Spirit of truth, is come, he shall guide you into all truth." While His own teaching had been partial, because of their weakness, the teaching of the apostles, under the promised Spirit, was to take in the whole sphere of God's truth.

So if we accept the authority of Christ we must accept that of the whole Bible, but we must, as already seen, accept Christ's authority.

2. Fulfilled Prophecies

The second reason I believe the Bible is the Word of God is because of its fulfilled prophecies.

There are two classes of prophecies in the Bible—first, the explicit, verbal prophecies; second, those of the types. In the first we have the definite prophecies concerning the Jews, the heathen nations, and the Messiah. Taking the prophecies regarding the Messiah as an illustration, look at Isaiah 53, Micah 5:2, Daniel 9:25–27. Many others might be mentioned, but these will serve as illustrations. In these prophecies, written hundreds of years before the Messiah came, we have the most explicit statements as to the manner and place of His birth, the manner of His reception by men, how His life would end, His resurrection, and His victory succeeding His death. When made, these prophecies were exceedingly improbable, and seemingly impossible of fulfillment; but they were fulfilled to the minutest detail of manner and place and time. How are we to account for it? Man could not have foreseen these improbable events—they lay hundreds of years ahead—but God could, and it is God who speaks through these men.

But the prophecies of the types are more remarkable still. Everything in the Old Testament—history, institutions, ceremonies—is prophetical. The high priesthood, the ordinary priesthood, the Levites, the prophets, priests and kings are all prophecies. The tabernacle, the brazen altar, the laver, the golden candlestick, the table of shewbread, the veil, the altar of incense, the ark of the covenant, the very coverings of the tabernacle, all serve as prophecies. In all these things, as we study them minutely and soberly in the light of the history of Jesus Christ and the church, we see—wrapped up in the ancient institutions ordained of God to meet an immediate purpose—prophecies of the death, atonement, and resurrection of Christ, the day of Pentecost, and the entire history of the church. We see the profoundest Christian doctrines of the New Testament clearly foreshadowed in these institutions of the Old Testament.

The only way in which you can appreciate this is to get into the Book itself and study all about the sacrifices and feasts, etc., till you see the truths of the New Testament shining out in the Old. If, in studying some elementary form of life, I find a rudimentary organ, useless now, but by the process of development to become of use in that animal's descendant, I say, back of this rudimentary organ is God, who, in the earlier animal, is preparing for the life and necessities of the animal that is to come. So, going back to these preparations in the Bible for the truth that is to be clearly taught at a later day, there is only one scientific way to account for them, namely, He who knows and prepares for the end from the beginning is the author of that Book.

3. The Unity of the Book

The third reason I believe the Bible is the Word of God is the unity throughout the Book.

This is an old argument, but a very satisfactory one. The Bible consists of sixty-six books, written by more than thirty different men, extending in the period of its composition over more than fifteen hundred years; written in three different languages, in many different countries, and by men on every plane of social life, from the herdsman and fisherman and cheap politician up to the king upon his throne. It is written under all sorts of circumstances. Yet in all this conglomeration we find an absolute unity of thought.

A wonderful thing about it is that this unity does not lie on the surface. On the surface there is oftentimes apparent contradiction, and the unity only comes out after deep and protracted study.

More wonderful yet is the organic character of this unity, beginning in the first book and growing till you come to its culmination in the last book of the Bible. We have first the seed, then the plant, then the bud, then the blossom, then the ripened fruit.

Suppose a vast building were to be erected, the stones for which were brought from the quarries in Rutland, Vermont; Berea, Ohio; Kasota, Minnesota; and Middletown, Connecticut. Each stone was hewn into final shape in the quarry from which it was brought. These stones were of all varieties of shape—cubical, rectangular, cylindrical, etc.—and size, but when they were brought together every stone fitted into its place, and when put together there rose before you a temple absolutely perfect in every outline, with its domes, sidewalls, buttresses, arches, transepts—not a gap or a flaw anywhere.

How would you account for it? You would say: "Back of these individual workers in the quarries was the mastermind of the architect who planned it all, and gave to each individual worker his specifications for the work."

So in this marvelous temple of God's truth, which we call the Bible, whose stones have been quarried at periods of time and in places so remote from one another, but where every smallest part fits each other part, we are forced to say that back of the human hands that wrought was the Master-mind that thought.

4. The Superiority of the Bible's Teaching

I believe the Bible is the Word of God for a fourth reason: the immeasurable superiority of the teachings of the Bible to those of any other and all other books.

It is quite fashionable in some quarters to compare the teachings of the Bible with the teachings of Zoroaster and Buddha, Confucius and Epictetus, Socrates, and Marcus Aurelius Antoninus, and a number of other heathen authors. The difference between the teachings of the Bible and those of these men is found in three points.

First, the Bible has in it nothing but truth, while all the others have truth mixed with error. It is true Socrates taught how a philosopher ought to die; he also taught how a woman of the town ought to conduct her business. Jewels there are in the teachings of these men, but (as Joseph Cook once said) they are "jewels picked out of the mud."

Second, the Bible contains *all* truth. There is not a truth to be found anywhere on moral or spiritual subjects that you cannot find in substance within the covers of that old Book. I have often, when speaking upon this subject, asked anyone to bring me a single truth on moral or spiritual subjects, which, upon reflection, I could not find within the covers of this Book, and no one has ever been able to do it. I have taken pains to compare some of the better teachings of infidels with those of the Bible. They indeed have jewels of thought, but they are, whether they knew it or not, stolen jewels, and stolen from the very Book they ridicule.

The *third* point of superiority is this: the Bible contains more truth than all other books together. Get together from all literature of ancient and modern times all the beautiful thoughts you can; put away all the rubbish; put all these truths that you have culled from the literature of all ages into one book, and as the result, even then you will not have a book that will take the place of this one Book.

This is not a large Book. I hold in my hand a copy that I carry in my vest pocket, and yet in this one little Book there is more of truth than in all the books that man has produced in all the ages of his history. How will you account for it? There is only one rational way. This is not man's book but God's Book.

5. Its Ability to Withstand Attacks

A fifth reason I accept the Bible as the Word of God is its ongoing victories over attack.

This Book has always been hated. No sooner was it given to the world than it met the hatred of men, and they tried to stamp it out. Celsus tried it by the brilliancy of his genius, Porphyry by the depth of his philosophy; but they failed. Lucian directed against it the shafts of his ridicule, Diocletian the power of the Roman Empire; but they failed. Edicts backed by all the power of the empire were issued that every Bible should be burned, and that everyone who had a Bible should be put to death. For eighteen centuries every engine of destruction that human science, philosophy, wit, reasoning, or brutality could bring to bear against a book has been brought to bear against that Book to stamp it out of the world, but it has a mightier hold on the world today than ever before.

If that were man's book, it would have been annihilated and forgotten hundreds of years ago, but because there is in it "the hiding of God's power," though at times all the great men of the world have been against it, and only an obscure remnant for it, still it has fulfilled wonderfully the words of Christ, though not in the sense of the original prophecy, "Heaven and earth shall pass away, but my word shall not pass away."

6. The Character of Those who Accept and Those Who Reject the Bible

A sixth reason I accept the Bible as the Word of God is on the ground of the character of those who accept and of those who reject the Book.

Two things speak for the divinity of the Bible—the character of those who accept it and, equally, the character of those who reject it. I do not mean by this that every man who professes to believe the Book is better than every man that does not, but show me a man living an unselfish, devoted life, one who without reservation has surrendered himself to do the will of God, and I will show you a man who believes the Bible to be God's Word. On the other hand, show me a man who rejects the divine authority of that Book, and I will show you a man living a life of greed, or lust, or spiritual pride, or self-will.

Suppose you have a book purporting to be by a certain author, and the people best acquainted with that author say it is his, and the people least acquainted with him say it is not. Which will you believe? Now, the people best acquainted with God say the Bible is His Book; those who are least acquainted with God say it is not. Which will you believe?

Furthermore, as men grow better they are more likely to accept the Bible, and as they grow worse they are more likely to reject it. We have all known men who were both sinful and unbelieving, who by forsaking their sin lost their unbelief. Did any of us ever know a man who was sinful and believing, who by forsaking his sin lost his faith? The nearer men live to God, the more confident they are that the Bible is God's Word; the farther they get away from Him, the more confident they are that it is not.

Where is the stronghold of the Bible? In the pure, unselfish, happy home. Where is the stronghold of infidelity? The gambling hall, the drinking saloon, and the brothel. If a man should walk into a saloon and lay a Bible down upon the bar, and order a drink, we should think there was a strange incongruity in his actions, but if he should lay any infidel writing upon the bar, and order a drink, we would not feel that there was any incongruity.

7. The Influence of the Bible

I believe the Bible is the Word of God for a seventh reason: the influence of the Book.

There is more power in that little Book to save men, and purify, gladden, and beautify their lives, than in all other literature put together—more power to lift men up to God. A stream never rises higher than its source, and a book that has a power to lift men up to God that no other book has, must have come down from God in a way that no other book has.

I have in mind as I write a man who was the most complete victim of strong drink I ever knew; a man of marvelous intellectual gifts, but who had been stupefied and brutalized and demonized by the power of sin, and he was an infidel. At last the light of God shone into his darkened heart, and by the power of that Book he has been transformed into one of the humblest, sweetest, noblest men I know today. What other book would have done that? What other book has the power to elevate not only individuals but communities and nations that this Book has?

8. The Inexhaustible Depth of the Bible

I believe the Bible is the Word of God for an eighth reason: the inexhaustible depth of the Book.

Nothing has been added to it in eighteen hundred years, yet a man like Bunsen or Neander cannot exhaust it by the study of a lifetime. George Mueller read it through more than one hundred times and said it was fresher every time he read it. Could that be true of any other book?

But more wonderful than this—not only individual men but generations of men for eighteen hundred years have dug into it and given to the world thousands of volumes devoted to its exposition, and they have not reached the bottom of the quarry yet. A book that man produces man can exhaust, but all men together have not been able to get to the bottom of this Book. How are you going to account for it? Only in this way—that in this Book are hidden the infinite and inexhaustible treasures of the wisdom and knowledge of God.

A brilliant Unitarian writer, in trying to disprove the inspiration of the Bible, says: "How irreligious to charge an infinite God with having written His whole Word in so small a book." He does not see how his argument can be turned against himself. What a testimony it is to the divinity of this Book that such infinite wisdom is stored away in so small a compass.

9. As We Grow in Knowledge and Holiness, We Grow toward the Bible

I believe the Bible is the Word of God for a ninth reason: as we grow in knowledge and holiness, we grow toward the Bible.

Every thoughtful person when he starts out to study the Bible finds many things with which he does not agree, but as he goes on studying and growing in likeness to God, the nearer he gets to God and the nearer he gets to the Bible. The nearer and nearer we get to God's standpoint, the less and less becomes the disagreement between us and the Bible. What is the inevitable mathematical conclusion? When we get where God is, we and the Bible will meet. In other words, the Bible was written from God's standpoint.

Suppose you are traveling through a forest under the conduct of an experienced and highly recommended guide. You come to a place where two roads diverge. The guide says the road to the left is the one to take, but your own judgment based upon the facts before you sees clear evidence that the road to the right is the one to take. You turn and say to the guide, "I know you have had large experience in this forest, and you have come to me highly recommended, but my own judgment tells me clearly that the road to the right is the one we should take, and I must follow my own judgment. I know my reason is not infallible, but it is the best guide I have."

But after you have followed that path for some distance, you are obliged to stop, turn around, and go back and take the path that the guide said was the right one.

After a while you come to another place where two roads diverge. Now the guide says the road to the right is the one to take, but your judgment clearly says the one to the left is the one to take, and again you follow your own judgment with the same result as before.

After you had this experience forty or fifty times, and found yourself wrong every time, I think you would have sense enough the next time to follow the guide.

That is just my experience with the Bible. I received it at first on the authority of others. Like almost all other young men, my confidence became shaken, and I came to the fork in the road more than forty times, and I followed my own reason, and in the outcome found myself wrong and the Bible right every time, and I trust that from this time on I shall have sense enough to follow the teachings of the Bible whatever my own judgment may say.

10. The Direct Testimony of the Holy Spirit

Finally, I believe the Bible is the Word of God based on the direct testimony of the Holy Spirit.

We began with God and shall end with God. We began with the testimony of the second person of the Trinity, and shall close with that of the third person of the Trinity.

The Holy Spirit sets His seal in the soul of every believer to the divine authority of the Bible. It is possible to get to a place where we need no argument to prove that the Bible is God's Word. Christ says, "My sheep hear my voice," and God's children know His voice, and I know that the voice that speaks to me from the pages of that Book is the voice of my Father. You will sometimes meet a pious old lady who tells you that she knows that the Bible is God's Word, and when you ask her for a reason for believing that it is God's Word, she can give you none. She simply says:

"I know it is God's Word."

You say: "That is mere superstition."

Not at all. She is one of Christ's sheep and recognizes her Shepherd's voice from every other voice. She is one of God's children and knows the voice that speaks to her from the Bible is the voice of God. She is above argument.

Everyone can have that testimony. John 7:17 (RV) tells you how to get it. "If any man willeth to do his will, he shall know of the teaching, whether it is of God." Just surrender your will to the will of God, no matter where it carries you, and you will put yourself in such an attitude toward God that when you read this book you will recognize that the voice that speaks to you from it is the voice of the God to whom you have surrendered your will.

Some time ago, when I was speaking to our students upon how to deal with skeptics, there was in the audience a graduate of a British University who had fallen into utter skepticism. At the close of the lecture he came to me and said:

"I don't wish to be discourteous, sir, but my experience contradicts everything you have said."

I asked him if he had followed the course of action that I had suggested and not found light. He said that he had. Stepping into another room, I had a pledge written out, running somewhat as follows:

"I believe there is an absolute difference between right and wrong, and I hereby take my stand upon the right, to follow it wherever it carries me. I promise earnestly to endeavor to find out what the truth is, and if I ever find that Jesus Christ is the Son of God, I promise to accept Him as my Savior and confess Him before the world."

I handed the paper to the gentleman and asked him if he was willing to sign it. He answered, "Certainly," and did sign it. I said to him:

"You don't know there is not a God, and you don't know that

God doesn't answer prayer. I know He does, but my knowledge cannot avail for you, but here is a possible clue to knowledge. Now you have promised to search earnestly for the truth, so you will follow this possible clue. I want you to offer a prayer like this: 'Oh, God, if there be any God, and Thou dost answer prayer, show me whether Jesus Christ is Thy Son, and if you show me He is, I will accept Him as my Savior and confess Him before the world.'"

This he agreed to do. I further requested that he would take the Gospel of John and read in it every day, reading only a few verses at a time slowly and thoughtfully, every time before he read asking God to give him light. This he also agreed to do, but he finished by saying, "There is nothing in it." However, at the end of a short time, I met him again, and he said to me, "There is something in that." I replied, "I knew that." Then he went on to say it seemed just as if he had been caught up by the Niagara River and had been carried along, and that before long he would be a shouting Methodist.

A short time ago I met this gentleman again, and he said to me that he could not understand how he had been so blind, how he had ever listened to the reasoning that he had; that it seemed to him utterly foolish now. I replied that the Bible would explain this to him, that the "natural man receiveth not the things of the Spirit of God," but that now he had put himself into the right attitude toward God and His truth, everything had been made plain. That man, who assured me that he was "a very peculiar man," and that methods that influenced others would not influence him, by putting himself into the right attitude toward God, got to a place where he received the direct testimony of the Holy Ghost that this Bible is God's Word; and anyone else can do the same.

Note

1. An audio recording from the archives of the Billy Graham Center, at Wheaton (Illinois) College, is available to download at the website http://www2.wheaton.edu/bgc/archives/docs/torreysermon.html.

2

How to Prepare a Sermon

AT THE PODIUM

Although not an actual sermon, Dr. Torrey here presents the rules of sermon preparation. It is interesting to see inside Torrey's sermon workshop, and also to compare these guidelines with his actual performance. This is a chapter from his large and influential "How-To" book on Christian ministry. Because it was written for publication in a book rather than for oral delivery, we might expect it to be written in a different tone of voice. But very early in his career, Torrey had already settled into a characteristic style that served equally well for speeches, sermons, tracts, and books.

SOURCE: R. A. Torrey, "How to Prepare a Sermon." *How to Work for Christ.* New York: Fleming H. Revell, 1901, 329–39.

There is no intention in this chapter of presenting an elaborate treatise on homiletics. It simply aims to give practical suggestions for the preparation of sermons that will win souls for Christ and edify believers.

First, Get Your Text or Subject

A great many neglect to do that, and when they get through preaching they do not know what they have been talking about, and neither does the audience. Never get up to speak without having something definite in your mind to speak about. There may be exceptions to that rule. There are times when one is called on suddenly to speak, and one has a right then to look to God for subject matter and manner of address. There are other times when one has made full preparation, but it becomes evident when he is about to speak that he must take up some other line of truth. In such a case also, one must depend upon God. But under ordinary circumstances, one should either have something definite in his mind that he is to speak about, or else keep silent.

It is true God has said in His Word, "Open thy mouth wide, and I will fill it" (Psalm 81:10), but this promise, as the context clearly shows, has nothing whatever to do with opening our mouth in speaking. Most people who take this promise as applying to their preaching, and who make their boast that they never prepare beforehand what they are going to say, when they open their mouths have them filled with anything but the wisdom of God. Christ did say to His disciples, "Take no thought how or what ye shall speak: for it shall be given you in that same hour what ye shall speak. For it is not ye that speak, but the Spirit of your Father which speaketh in you" (Matthew 10:19–20); but this promise did not have to do with preaching but with witnessing for Christ in circumstances of emergency and peril. In all cases of similar emergency, we have a right to rest in the same promise, and we have a right also to take the spirit of it as applying to our preaching. But if one has an opportunity to prepare for the services before him, and neglects that opportunity, God will not set a premium upon his laziness and neglect, by giving him a sermon in his time of need.

How shall we select our text or subject?

1. *Ask God for it.* The best texts and topics are those that a man gets on his knees. No one should ever prepare a sermon without first going alone with God, and there definitely seeking His wisdom in the choice of a text or topic.

2. *Keep a text book.* I do not mean the kind that you buy but the kind that you make for yourself. Have a small book that you can carry in your vest pocket, and as subjects or texts occur to you in your regular study of the Word, or in hearing others preach, or in conversation with people, jot them down in your book. Oftentimes texts will come to you when you are riding on the street cars or going about your regular work. If so, put them down at once.

It is said that Ralph Waldo Emerson would sometimes be heard at night stumbling around his room in the dark. When his wife would ask him what he was doing, he would reply that he had a thought and he wanted to pin it. Oftentimes when you are reading a book, a text will come to you that is not mentioned in the book at all. Indeed, one of the best ways to get to thinking is to take up some book that stimulates thought. It will set your own mental machinery in operation. Not that you are going to speak on anything in that particular book, but it sets you to thinking, and your thought goes out along the line on which you are going to speak. Very often while listening to a sermon, texts or subjects or sermon points will come to your mind. I do not mean that you will take the points of the preacher, though you may sometimes do that if you will thoroughly digest them and make them your own, but something that he says will awaken a train of thought in your own mind. I rarely hear a man preach but his sermon suggests many sermons to me.

Put but one text or subject on a page of your textbook. Then when points or outlines come to you, jot them down under the proper text or subject. In this way you will be accumulating material for future use. After a while texts and topics and outlines will multiply so rapidly that you will never be able to catch up with them and will never be at a loss for something to preach about.

3. *Expound a book in order.* Take a book of the Bible and expound it. You should be very careful about this, however, or you will be insufferably dry. One of the best preachers in an eastern state undertook to expound one of the long books of the Bible. He made it so dry that some of his congregation said they were going to stay away from church until he got through that book; they were thoroughly tired of it. Study the masters in this line of work; men like Alexander Maclaren, William H. Taylor, and Horatius Bonar. F. B. Meyer's expositions on Abraham, Jacob, Elijah, Moses, etc., are very suggestive.

4. *Read the Bible in course, and read until you come to a text that you wish to use.* This was George Mueller's plan, and he is a safe man to follow. He was wonderfully used of God. When the time drew near to preach a sermon, he would take up the Bible and open it to the place where he was reading at that time, first going down upon his knees and asking God to give him a text, and then he would read on and on and on until he came to the desired text.

Second, Find Your Points

I do not say make your points. Find them. Find them in your text, or if you are preaching on a topic, find them in the various texts in the Bible that bear upon that topic. It is desirable often to preach on a topic instead of on a single text. Never write a sermon and then hunt up a text for it. That is one of the most wretched and outrageous things that a man who believes that the Bible is the Word of God can do. It is simply using the Word of God as a label or endorsement for your idea. We are ambassadors for Christ, with a message. Our message is in the Word of God, and we have no right to prepare our own message, and then go to the Word of God merely to get a label for it.

How shall we find our points?

Begin with *a careful analysis of the text.* Write down one by one the points contained in the text. Suppose for example your text is

Acts 13:38–39: "Be it known unto you therefore, men and brethren, that through this man is preached unto you the forgiveness of sins: And by him all that believe are justified from all things, from which ye could not be justified by the law of Moses."

By an analysis of the text, you will find the following points taught in it:

1. Forgiveness is preached unto us.
2. This may be known (not merely surmised, or guessed, or hoped, or believed).
3. It is known by the resurrection of Christ (this comes out in the "therefore" and the context). Forgiveness is not a mere hope but a certainty resting upon a solid and uncontrovertible fact. The one who here speaks had seen the risen Christ.
4. This forgiveness is through Jesus Christ. In developing this point, the question will arise and should be answered, How is forgiveness through Jesus Christ?
5. Everyone who believeth is forgiven. Under this point there will be four special points:
   a. He is forgiven (not shall be).
   b. Every one that believeth is forgiven.
   c. He is forgiven all things.
   d. The meaning of justified.

Next, *ask questions about the text*. For example, suppose you take Matthew 11:28 as a text: "Come unto me, all ye that labour and are heavy laden, and I will give you rest." You might ask questions on that text as follows:

1. Who are invited?
2. What is the invitation?
3. What will be the result of accepting the invitation?

4. What will be the result of rejecting the invitation?

One of the easiest and simplest ways of preaching is to take a text and ask questions about it that you know will be in the minds of your hearers, and then answer these questions. If you are preaching upon a subject, you can ask and answer questions regarding the subject. Suppose, for example, that you are to preach upon the subject of the new birth; you could ask the following questions and give Bible answers to them, and thus prepare an excellent sermon:

1. What is it to be born again?
2. Is the new birth necessary?
3. Why is it necessary?
4. What are the results of being born again?
5. How can one be born again?

If you answer the questions that suggest themselves to your own mind, you will probably answer the questions that suggest themselves to the minds of others. Imagine your congregation to be a lot of interrogation points. Take up their questions and answer them, and you will interest them.

Finally, *if you are going to preach upon a topic, go through the Bible on that topic and write down the various texts that bear upon it.*

As you look these texts over, they will naturally fall under different subdivisions. These subdivisions will be your principal points. For example, suppose you are going to preach on "Prayer." Some of the passages on prayer will come under the head of "The Power of Prayer"; that can be your first main point. Others will come under the head of "How to Pray"; that will be your second main point, with doubtless many subordinate points. Other passages will come under the head of "Hindrances to Prayer," and this will make your third main point.

Third, Select among Your Points

After finding your points, the next thing is to select them. You will seldom be able to take up all the points that you find in a text, or upon a topic, unless you preach much longer than the average congregation will stand. Few ministers can wisely preach longer than thirty or forty minutes. To a person just beginning to preach, twenty minutes is often long enough and sometimes too long. At a cottage meeting fifteen minutes is certainly long enough, and usually too long. The more you study a subject, the more points you will get, and it is a great temptation to give the people all these points. They have all been helpful to you, and you wish to give them all out to them, but you must bear in mind that the great majority of your congregation will not be so interested in truth as you are. You must strenuously resist the temptation to tell people everything you know. You will have other opportunities to give the rest of the points if you give well the few that you now select; but if you attempt to tell all that you know in a single sermon, you will never have another chance.

In selecting your points, the question is not which points are the best in the abstract but which are best to give to your particular congregation, at this particular time. In preaching on a given text, it will be wise to use certain points at one time and certain other points at another time. The question is, which are the points that will do the most good and be the most helpful to your congregation on this special occasion.

Fourth, Arrange Your Points

There is a great deal in the arrangement of your points. Many preachers have good points in their sermons, but they do not make them in a good order. They begin where they ought to end, and end where they ought to begin. What may be the right order at one time may not be the right way at another time. There are, however, a few suggestions that may prove helpful:

1. *Make your points in logical order.* Put those first that come first in thought. There are many exceptions to this rule. If our purpose in preaching is not to preach a good sermon but to win souls, a point will often be more startling and produce more effect out of its logical order than in it.

2. *Do not make your strongest points first and then taper down to the weakest.* If some points are weaker than others, it is best to lead along up to a climax. If a point is really weak, it is best to leave it out altogether.

3. *Put that point last that leads to the important decision that you have in view in your sermon.* It may not in itself be the strongest point, but it is the one that leads to action; therefore, put it last in order that it may not be forgotten before the congregation are called upon to take the action that you have in mind.

4. *Give your points in such a way that the first leads naturally to the second, and the second to the third, and the third to the fourth, etc.* This is of great importance in speaking without notes. It is quite possible to so construct a sermon that when one has once gotten well under way, everything that follows comes so naturally out of what precedes it that one may deliver the whole sermon without any conscious effort of memory. When you have selected your points and written them down, look at them attentively and see which point would naturally come first, and then ask yourself which one of the remaining points this would naturally suggest. When you have chosen the two, in the same way select the third, and so on.

Fifth, Plan Your Introduction

One of the most important parts of the sermon is the introduction. The two most important parts are the introduction and conclusion. The middle is of course important; do not understand me to say you should have a strong introduction and conclusion and disregard all that lies between, but it is of the very first importance that you begin well and end well. In the introduction you get the attention of the people; in the conclusion you get the decisive results; so you should be especially careful about these. You must catch the attention of people first of all. This you should do by your first few sentences, by the very first sentence you utter if possible.

How shall we do this? Sometimes by a graphic description of the circumstances of the text. Mr. Moody was peculiarly gifted along this line. He would take a Bible story and make it live right before you. Sometimes it is well to introduce a sermon by speaking of some interesting thing that you have just heard or seen—some incident that you have read in the paper, some notable picture that you have seen in a gallery, some recent discovery of science. In one sermon that I often preach, and that has been used of God to the conversion of many, I usually begin by referring to a remarkable picture I once saw in Europe. I start out by saying, "I once saw a picture that made an impression upon my mind that I have never forgotten." Of course everybody wants to know about that picture. I do not care anything about the picture; I only use it to secure the attention of people and thus lead directly up to the subject.

If you have several good stories in your sermon, it is wise to tell one of the very best at the start. Sometimes a terse and striking statement of the truth that you are going to preach will startle people and awaken their attention at the very outset. Sometimes it is well to jump right into the heart of your text or subject, making some crisp and striking statements, thus causing everybody to prick up their ears and think, "Well, I wonder what is coming next."

Sixth, Illustrate Your Points

Illustrate every point in the sermon. It will clinch the matter, and fasten it in a person's mind. Think up good illustrations, but do not over-illustrate. One striking and impressive illustration will fasten the point.

Seventh, Arrange Your Conclusion

How shall we conclude a sermon? The way to conclude a sermon is to sum up and apply what you have been saying. One can usually learn more as to how to close a sermon by listening to a lawyer in court than he can by listening to the average preacher in a pulpit. Preachers aim too much at delivering a perfect discourse, while a lawyer aims at carrying his case. The sermon should close with application and personal appeal. It is a good thing to close a Gospel sermon with some striking incident, an incident that touches men's hearts and makes them ready for action. I have often heard men preach a sermon, and right in the middle they would tell some striking story that melted and moved people, then they would go on to the close without any incident whatever. If they had only told the story at the close, the sermon would have been much more effective. It would have been better still if they had had that moving story in the middle, and another just as good or better at the close.

A true sermon does not exist for itself. This, as has already been hinted, is the great fault with many of our modern sermonizers. The sermon exists for itself as a work of art, but it is not worth anything in the line of doing good. As a work of rhetorical art it is perfect, but as a real sermon it is a total failure. What did it accomplish? A true sermon exists for the purpose of leading someone to Christ or building someone up in Christ. I have heard people criticize some preachers, and say that they broke nearly all the rules of rhetoric and of homiletics, and that the sermon was a failure, when the sermon had accomplished its purpose and brought many to the acceptance of Christ. Again, I have heard people say, "What a magnificent sermon we have just heard!" and I have asked, "What good did it do you?" and they would say, "I do not know as it did me any good." I have further asked, what good it did anyone else, what there was in it that would particularly benefit anyone. It was a beautiful sermon, but it was a beautiful fraud.

A few years ago a well-known professor of homiletics went to hear Mr. Moody preach. He afterward told his class that Mr. Moody violated every law of homiletics. Perhaps he did, but he won souls to Christ by the thousands and tens of thousands, more souls, probably, in one year than that professor of homiletics ever won to Christ in his whole lifetime. A scientific angler will get a fishing rod of remarkable lightness and elasticity, a reel of the latest pattern, a silk line of the finest texture, flies of the choicest assortment, and he will go to the brook and throw out his line with the most wonderful precision. The fly falls where he planned that it should, but he does not catch anything. A little boy comes along with a freshly cut willow stick for a rod, a piece of tow string for a line, a bent pin for a hook, and angleworms for bait. He throws out his line without any theoretic knowledge of the art and pulls in a speckled trout. The boy is the better fisher. The man has a perfect outfit and is wonderfully expert in throwing his line, but he does not catch anything.

A good deal of our pretended fishing for men is of the same character. Let us never forget that we are fishers for men, and our business is to catch men alive for Christ. Let us not try to save our sermons but to save men's souls.

A Final Word: Never Read a Sermon

I would not advise you to write your sermons out, because what you have written might afterward enslave you, but I would advise you to do a great deal of writing, not for the sake of preaching what you have written, but for the sake of improving your style. Most emphatically would I advise you never to read a sermon. The more preachers I listen to, the more firmly convinced do I become that a sermon ought never to be read. Of course, there are advantages in writing the sermon out and reading it, but they are counterbalanced many times over by the disadvantages. I once heard a man deliver an address, who said before beginning, that as he wished to say a great deal in a very short time, he had written his address. It was a magnificent address, but he had no freedom of delivery, and the audience did not get it at all. As far as practical results were concerned, it would have been a great deal better if he had said less and spoken without his manuscript. Furthermore, it is not true that a man can say more without a manuscript than he can with it. Anyone who really has a call to preach can train himself to speak just as freely as he writes. He can be just as logical. He can pack his sermon as full of matter and argument. His style can be just as faultless. It will be necessary, however, that he should think out closely beforehand just what he is going to say.

After thinking your sermon all out carefully, when you come to preach, your mind will naturally follow the lines along which you have been thinking. You set the mental machinery going, and it will go of itself. The mind is just as much a creature of habit as any part of our body, and after one has thought consecutively and thoroughly along a certain line, when he takes up that thought again, his mind naturally runs in the grooves that have been cut out.

PART 2

THE GREAT WORLD TOUR

INTRODUCTION

The Evangelical Magellan

When Torrey announced that the death of Moody was a call to move forward, he seemed to have discerned something in God's purposes that others were missing. The prayer groups Torrey had formed continued to grow, and before long he received a call to preach in Australia. Taking with him song leader Charles Alexander, Torrey began, at age forty-five, an evangelistic journey that would take him around the world in the next few years. The Torrey-Alexander revival started out in Hawaii and Japan, but when Torrey hit Australia, his preaching began to attract enormous crowds. The audiences in Australia, New Zealand, India, England, Scotland, Ireland, Wales, and numerous places in Europe were all electrified by the revival. Their meetings became the biggest news item in most of the cities they came to. It is worth remembering that this Torrey-Alexander juggernaut was in motion during the years immediately before the (not directly related) Welsh Revival of 1904, the Azusa Revival of 1906, and the Pyongyang Revival of 1907.

What was so powerful about the Torrey-Alexander presentations? One of the keys was that Torrey presented himself as intellectually credible and serious, with a message that spoke directly to the mind of his listeners as well as their hearts. Reuben A. Torrey was well educated and respectably dressed; one friend noted that he *often* wore a tall hat, but *always* spoke as if he were wearing a tall hat. The typical R. A. Torrey sermon was a list of reasons or arguments, briskly stated and vigorously argued, driving toward one conclusion.

One of the best examples is his sermon "How God Has Blockaded the Road to Hell," reprinted in his *Revival Addresses.* (A version of this classic sermon is included in chapter 8, "God's Blockade of the Road to Hell.") Torrey begins with direct address to his hearers:

> If any man or woman in this audience is lost, it won't be God's fault. God does not wish you to be lost. God longs to have you saved. God has filled the path of sin the road that leads to hell with obstacles. He has made it hard and bitter. God has filled it full of obstacles, and you cannot go on in it without surmounting one obstacle after another. I am to talk to you tonight about some of the obstacles that God has put in the path of sin and ruin.[1]

The rest of the sermon is a list of ways in which God has blockaded the road to sin and hell:

> Number 1. Godly parents. They are a good influence on you, but you ignore them and seek your own way.
> Number 2. Christian influence in your country. It surrounds you on all sides, but you persist in sin.
> Number 3. This sermon. It is being spoken in your presence and applied to your conscience. Do not seek to climb over this barricade.
> Number 4. The Bible. You know what it says. Etc.

Torrey would hammer away at his audience in this manner for some time, and then give the meeting to his song leader, Charles Alexander, who would lead congregational singing. The typical hymn was a rather treacly Victorian song about heaven, mother, and the old-time religion. A song that even Alexander was hesitant to use was "Tell Mother I'll Be There." But once he did sing it, the audience responded so powerfully that he made it a normal part of the repertoire.[2] Here are some key lyrics:

When I was but a little child, how well I recollect
How I would grieve my mother with my folly and neglect;
And now that she has gone to Heav'n I miss her tender care:
O Savior, tell my mother I'll be there!
Tell mother I'll be there, in answer to her prayer;
This message, blessed Savior, to her bear!
Tell mother I'll be there, Heav'n's joys with her to share
Yes, tell my darling mother I'll be there.[3]

It is hard for us in the twenty-first century to understand why these songs were so popular at that time, and especially why they were so powerful as a religious expression. In the context of an R. A. Torrey sermon, however, an Alexander song was the occasion of a great many people responding wholeheartedly to the call of the Gospel. Torrey would hammer away with logic and argument, appealing to the mind, and then Alexander would go straight for the heart. The sermon-and-song combination could be viewed cynically as an alternation of bullying and manipulating. But the more than 100,000 souls who came to Christ through this revival understood it otherwise. They heard in the Torrey-Alexander campaign the call of a Savior who spoke through these men to their minds and their hearts alike, calling them back to a faith that was just beginning to fade from their lives but was lurking powerfully in their cultural heritage.

In many cities, Torrey and Alexander displayed a huge banner that said simply "Get Right with God." This four-word exhortation was enough for their audiences: they knew that their modern, secularizing lives were breaking the hearts of their saintly mothers, they knew where the churches were and what they would hear there, and they knew deep down that their great need was to get right with God. The Torrey-Alexander campaign was just the occasion for it, and what an occasion it was. Their Gospel campaign spanned three continents (Asia, Australia, and Europe) during Torrey's travels from 1902 to 1905.

As the Torrey-Alexander tours continued, there was great demand for printed versions of Torrey's sermons. He published them as fast as he could, and the volumes sold well for many years. Torrey's influence spread as the sermons became a model for preachers who were impressed with the practical results of his work.

Notes

1. R. A. Torrey, "God's Blockade on the Road to Hell," *Real Salvation and Whole-Hearted Service* (New York: Revell, 1905), 60.
2. Helen C. Alexander, *Charles Alexander* (New York: Marshall Brothers), 1921, 65.
3. Charles M. Alexander and Edwin Bookmyer, *Alexander's Hymns* (Philadelphia, Sterling Music, 1921), 195. In public domain.

3

Found Wanting

AT THE PODIUM

The sermons Torrey preached on his great evangelistic and revival tours have a special character. They are especially sharp and pointed, uniquely confrontational. They are not especially doctrinal, nor are they expositions of extended passages of Scripture. In fact, in this message Torrey hangs the entire sermon on one word, and that word in Aramaic: TEKEL, "found wanting" (from a message given to Babylon's Belshazzar in Daniel 5). This may seem like a modest foundation for a sermon, and it may also seem to depart from Torrey's own stated principles in the previous chapter. But in fact as the sermon develops, it becomes clear that the idea of being evaluated by God's Word is just an introduction to his exposition of God's law as stated in the Ten Commandments.

Source: R. A. Torrey. "Found Wanting." *Revival Addresses.* New York: Revell, 1903, 30–48.

Anyone who loves drama should read the Bible, for the Bible is the most dramatic book ever written. There is nothing to compare with it in Aeschylus or Sophocles or Euripides among the ancients, or in Shakespeare among the moderns, in striking situations, in graphic delineation, and in startling *dénouement.*

One of the most intensely interesting and at the same time suggestive scenes in the Bible is that described in Daniel 5—Belshazzar's feast. Belshazzar was not the supreme king of Babylon. Nabonidus, his father, was king, and had associated him with himself on the throne; Belshazzar was second ruler in the kingdom. The critics used to tell us there never was such a king as Belshazzar; but Sir William Rawlinson dug up a tablet from Nabonidus himself, on which he speaks of his son Belshazzar; and again the critics, as so often before, were brought to grief by the discoveries of modern archaeology.

But now Belshazzar is in supreme command in the city. His father, Nabonidus, had been shut outside the city walls by the forces of Cyrus. Puffed up by the pride of his newly gotten power, Belshazzar makes a great banquet. The palace is a blaze of light. The long tables are set for more than a thousand guests. They are brilliant and dazzling with plates and cups and tankards of silver and gold, many-jeweled, reflecting back the light from countless candelabra. Reclining at the tables are the guests, with fingers and arms ringed and jeweled. The air is heavy with perfume and tremulous with the music of harp and dulcimer and sackbut. Between the tables the oriental women weave through the contortions and distortions of the Asiatic dance. Back and forth across the tables fly jest and repartee.

In the midst of this hilarity, a strange and daring conceit enters the mind of the royal entertainer. Belshazzar whispers to his chief steward a secret command. The guests are all agog with curiosity to know what the mysterious mandate may be. Their curiosity is soon gratified; for the chief steward, followed by a host of retainers, comes in bearing in their arms the cups of gold and silver that Nebuchadnezzar had carried away from the temple of Jehovah after sacking the city of Jerusalem. Belshazzar commands that the cups be filled with Babylonian wine and passed from lip to lip—while he and his guests sing the praises of gods of gold and of silver, of brass, of iron, of wood, and of stone.

The Mysterious Fingers

The hilarity becomes more boisterous. Louder and louder thrum the instruments, faster and faster spin the feet of the dancers, swifter and swifter fly jest and repartee. Suddenly a hush like death falls upon the banqueting hall. One of the revelers, lifting his eyes to the wall, sees the fingers of a man's hand writing. As he gazes in wonder he becomes the center of observation, and all eyes turn in the same direction.

Now the king turns and looks also. There, writing in characters of fire, are the mysterious fingers of an armless hand. Terror freezes Belshazzar to the very soul. In the graphic language of the prophet Daniel, "the king's countenance was changed, and his thoughts troubled him, so that the joints of his loins were loosed, and his knees smote one against another" (5:6). In a few moments Belshazzar pulls himself together and hoarsely cries, "Bring in the astrologers, the Chaldeans, and the soothsayers."

In come the magi of Babylon, splendidly appareled, with proud and stately tread. Expectation rises high in their hearts. They think that by their cunning arts they can deceive the king and gain new emoluments, but only for a moment. The look of confidence fades from their faces. The writing is beyond their art.

Again terror lays hold on Belshazzar. Again his countenance was changed in him. The queen mother hears the confusion. She walks in with stately tread and tries to reassure her royal son. "O king, live for ever: let not thy thoughts trouble thee, nor let thy countenance be changed: there is a man in thy kingdom, in whom is the spirit of the holy gods." And she proceeds to sing the praises of Daniel. "Let Daniel be called, and he will shew the interpretation" (vv. 10, 12). Daniel is summoned. Belshazzar turns to him and says:

> I have heard of thee, that the spirit of the gods is in thee, and that light and understanding and excellent wisdom is

> found in thee. . . . And I have heard of thee, that thou canst make interpretations, and dissolve doubts: now if thou canst read the writing, and make known to me the interpretation thereof, thou shalt be clothed with scarlet, and have a chain of gold about thy neck, and shalt be the third ruler in the kingdom. (vv. 14 , 16)

Daniel, with noble pride, scorns the proffered gifts. "Let thy gifts be to thyself, and give thy rewards to another; yet I will read the writing unto the king, and make known to him the interpretation." But first Daniel proceeds to rebuke the blasphemous daring of Belshazzar. He recalls the history of Nebuchadnezzar, his grandfather, and how God had humbled his stouthearted pride. Then he says,

> The God in whose hand thy breath is, and whose are all thy ways, hast thou not glorified: Then was the part of the hand sent from him; and this writing was written. And this is the writing that was written, MENE, MENE, TEKEL, UPHARSIN. This is the interpretation of the thing: MENE; God hath numbered thy kingdom, and finished it. TEKEL; Thou art weighed in the balances, and art found wanting. PERES; Thy kingdom is divided, and given to the Medes and Persians. (vv. 23–28)

Belshazzar calls for the royal robe, and it is placed on Daniel. A chain of gold is cast about his neck, and he is proclaimed next to Belshazzar, third ruler in the kingdom. The royal banquet goes on. The hilarity increases; but, hark! the tramp, tramp, tramp, tramp of withers' feet in the streets of Babylon. The armies of Cyrus have turned the waters of the Euphrates, and have come in by the riverbed and the two-leaved gates of Babylon.

A Crashing at the Gate

There is a crashing sound at the gate. The guests look round for a place to flee. But it is too late. Tramp, tramp, tramp, up the palace stairs, with a crash and a rush, the Persian and Median soldiers came in. Swords flash in air for a moment. Belshazzar looks up and sees the sword over his head. It falls. Belshazzar is a corpse. "That night was Belshazzar the king of the Chaldeans slain" (v. 30).

I call your attention to one word on the wall: "TEKEL; Thou art weighed in the balances, and art found wanting."

In whose balances was Belshazzar weighed? The balances of God. Not in the balances of his own estimation of himself: he would never have been found wanting there. Not in the balances of public opinion: the men of Babylon would have said, "Belshazzar is the greatest of our statesmen, and the coming man." Not in the balances of human philosophy. In the balances of God.

Every man and woman here tonight is to be weighed in the same balances, the balances of God. How much do you suppose that you weigh in the balances of God? I do not ask you how much you weigh in your own opinion of yourself. That is of no consequence, for many a man who thinks most of himself is of least account in the mind of God. I do not ask how much you weigh in the balances of public opinion. You may be a leading citizen and a chief magistrate, whom all delight to honor; but oftentimes that which is highly esteemed among men is abomination in the sight of God.

How much do you think you weigh in the balances of God? There are some of us who set much store by our morality, our culture, and our refinement; but if we knew how little we weighed in the balances of the eternal and all holy God, we would fall on our knees and cry, "God be merciful to me a sinner."

How God Weighs Us

Is there any way in which we can tell how much we weigh in the balances of God? There is. God has given to us the weights wherewith He weighs us.

Turn to Exodus 20 and you will get the first ten weights by which God weighs men—the well-known Ten Commandments. Let me read them.

"Thou shalt have no other gods before me." What is a man's god? A man's god is the thing he thinks most of. If a man thinks more of money than anything else, money is his god; and many a citizen of Edinburgh worships Plutus, the god of wealth. Many a man is sacrificing conscience, sacrificing honor, and sacrificing obedience to God to gain money. You do things in business that you know are not according to the teachings of the Bible, things that you know are not pleasing to a holy God, because there is money in them. Gold is your god, and you are found wanting by the first of God's commandments. There are men who worship gold just as if they had a sovereign hung up in their bedchamber, and said their prayers to it.

Many worship social position. How many are doing things in matters of dress and in matters of social life that are disapproved by conscience! But it is what society does, and they think that if they do not do the same, they will lose their position in society. You are putting society before God. Society is your god. You are weighed and found wanting by the first of God's laws.

Major Whittle once went, in Washington, to call upon a man who had been prominent in public and church life. He was showing Major Whittle over his beautiful new house. They came to a large and beautiful room, and Major Whittle asked, "What is this for?"

The man was silent at first. "What is this for?" asked Major Whittle again.

The man hung his head and said, "Well, Major, if you must know, this is a ballroom."

"What! A ballroom? Do you mean to tell me that you have sunk so low that you have a ballroom in your house?"

"Well, Major, I never thought I would come to this; but my wife and daughter said we were in society now, that this was the thing in Washington, and that we must have it to keep our position in Washington society."

Social position was their god, and that man paid for it dearly in the wreck and ruin of his home.

Many a man worships whisky. How many a man is sacrificing his brainpower, his business capacity, the respect of his fellow citizens, the reverence of his wife and children, in devotion to the cursed whisky. I saw many a hideous god when I was traveling in India, all sorts of beastly images that men bow down before and worship, but I know no god more beastly, no god more disgusting than this god of whisky, upon the altar of which men are offering as a sacrifice their children and their interests.

How many a young man and young woman worship the god of pleasure. They are doing things for pleasure that their conscience disapproves of, things that hinder communion with God. They are sacrificing everything that they may have amusement and pleasure. Amusement is their god. Weighed and found wanting by the first weight of the Ten Commandments.

I have no time to dwell upon the second command: "Thou shalt not make unto thee any graven image, or any likeness of any thing that is in heaven above, or that is in the earth beneath, or that is in the water under the earth: Thou shalt not bow down thyself to them, nor serve them: for I the Lord thy God am a jealous God, visiting the iniquity of the fathers upon the children unto the third and fourth generation of them that hate me; and shewing mercy unto thousands of them that love me, and keep my commandments."

Profaning God's Name

The third commandment reads, "Thou shalt not take the name of the Lord thy God in vain; for the Lord will not hold him guiltless that taketh his name in vain." How much do you weigh when you are weighed by that law? Oh, how many a man on your streets breaks that law! And men not only break it, but they think it a light matter. They think that law is of no consequence. When you approach men and speak to them about Christ, they will say, "Well, but I do not know that I need Christ. I am not a very bad man. I have never stolen anything. I have never killed anybody. I have never committed adultery. Oh, I do swear occasionally." They think it a light matter, but God does not regard it so, saying, "The Lord will not hold him guiltless that taketh his name in vain."

If there is any sin which shows that the very foundations of a man's character are honeycombed and rotten, it is the sin of profanity. You cannot trust a profane swearer anywhere. A profane swearer is ripe for any crime. What is the only foundation for a sound character? Reverence for God, and when that is gone the foundation of character is gone. Character may not crumble away at once, as a building does not always fall the moment its foundation is rotten, in a measure, but it will fall. The foundation is gone. No man can swear profanely until he has gotten very, very low in the moral scale.

A man has to go down pretty low (has he not?) to speak disrespectfully of his mother. We have seen men go pretty far into sin, and yet have so much manhood left that when others spoke insultingly about their mother, they would resent it. A man has fallen very low who will speak lightly of his mother, but a man has got immeasurably lower before he will speak profanely of God. The purest mother is nothing to the all holy One. No mother ever loved a child, no mother ever sacrificed for a child, as God has loved you and made sacrifices for you; and if you can take God's name upon your lips in profanity, you are a vile wretch. I beseech of you get on your face before the eternal God before you sleep and cry to Him for mercy.

But there are other ways of taking God's name in vain besides profane swearing. Much that we call praying is taking God's name in vain. Every time you have knelt down to pray and have had no thought of God in your heart while you take His name upon your lips, you have taken God's name in vain. In the Church of England you go through those marvelously beautiful prayers in the ritual, but when you do it as a mere matter of form, with no thought of God in your mind, you have taken God's name in vain. You repeat that wonderful prayer that the Master Himself taught us: "Our Father which art in heaven, hallowed be thy name. Thy kingdom come. Thy will be done in earth, as it is in heaven. Give us this day our daily bread. And forgive us our debts, as we forgive our debtors. And lead us not into temptation, but deliver us from evil: For thine is the kingdom, and the power, and the glory, for ever." All the time you recite it you have not one thought what you are saying. It is downright appalling profanity.

Honoring God and Your Parents

The fourth command tells us to "remember the sabbath day, to keep it holy. Six days shalt thou labour, and do all thy work: But the seventh day is the sabbath." This is not the seventh day of the week, as some men say, daring to put into God's Word what He did not put in, but the seventh day is for rest after six days of work, without specifying which day of the week it should come. Of course it was the seventh day of the week with the Jew, in commemoration of the old creation; but with the Christian it is the first day of the week, in commemoration of the new creation through a risen Lord. "The seventh day is the sabbath of the Lord thy God: in it thou shalt not do any work, thou, nor thy son, nor thy daughter, thy manservant, nor thy maidservant, nor thy cattle, nor thy stranger that is within thy gates: For in six days the Lord made heaven and earth, the sea, and all that in them is, and rested the seventh day: wherefore the Lord blessed the sabbath day, and hallowed it" (vv. 10–11).

There was a day when Scotsmen kept that law. It may be you do now; but, alas, in India I saw a thing that stirred my blood and sickened my heart. I saw Scotsmen—not merely Englishmen and Irishmen—I saw Scotsmen, from the land of the Covenanters, on God's holy day, not in the house of God but off playing golf, riding on their wheels, engaging in all manner of amusement. I do not know whether you do it at home or not; but the land, the city, the individual who forgets the Sabbath day has undermined the foundations of God's favor and its own prosperity.

The fifth command tells us to "honour thy father and thy mother: that thy days may be long upon the land which the Lord thy God giveth thee." I wish I had time to dwell upon that; for we are getting into a day when the young think they know more than their parents, speaking lightly about "the old man" and "the old woman." They think father and mother are old fogies, and that the young people know it all. They disobey their parents. The child who disobeys a parent will bring upon his own head the curse of God. There is only one law superior to the law of father and mother, and that is the law of God. Even those who are grown up, and do not treat the father and mother with the respect and consideration that they should, will reap what they sow. God have mercy upon the one, young or old, who breaks that commandment.

The Many Ways We May Murder

The sixth command is, "Thou shalt not kill." How much do you weigh by that law? You say, "I am all right by that law. We have no murderers here." Are you absolutely sure? "Why, certainly. Where do you think you are talking? Down in the Grassmarket?" No, I am talking in the Synod Hall, but there are other ways of killing people besides driving a dagger into their heart or firing a bullet into their brain. A husband can kill his wife by neglect, and cruelty, and unfaithfulness. How many a woman is hastening to an early grave, with a broken heart, because she has learned that the man who swore to be true to her is unfaithful.

One day I was talking with a very brilliant man, who was under the influence of liquor. I said to him, "John, you ought to take Jesus Christ." "Oh," was his reply, "you know I do not believe as you do. I am one of these new theologians. I have a broader theology than you have. I am one of those believers in the eternal hope. You do not believe that old-fashioned theology, do you? Now, honestly, suppose I should drop right down here now, what would become of me?"

I said, "John, you would go straight to hell, and you would deserve to go."

"What have I done?"

"I will tell you. You have got your wife's heart under your heel, and you are grinding the life out of it. What is worse, you are trampling underfoot the Christ of God, who died on the cross of Calvary to save you."

How many a son is killing his mother by his wild, dissolute life. I remember staying in a beautiful home, where there was everything that wealth could buy. One would have thought that the mistress of that home must be a perfectly happy woman. But she would rise in the middle of the night, and walk up and down the halls of her beautiful home with a breaking heart. A few months after, she died. Why? She had a wandering boy. She did not even know where he was; and as I stood by her grave, with that wandering boy, who had come to her dying bed, I thought in my heart, "Murdered by her wayward son."

Some of you are hastening your mother's footsteps to the grave. You have not written your mother for six months. In Melbourne a man came rushing down the hall and said, "Oh, I have killed my mother." He rushed into the inquiry room and was led to Christ. Is there a man here who is killing his mother? Repent, take

Christ; write to your mother tonight that you are saved.

There are other ways of murdering people. I do not know whether it is common in Scotland. I think, and I certainly hope, not. But it is common where Scotsmen have gone. How shall I describe it? The most appalling kind of murder in the world. Mothers murdering their own helpless babes, to escape the responsibility of what is one of the greatest privileges in the world, a large family. If there is any hand in the world that is scarlet with the blood of murder, it is that of the woman who murders her own unborn babe; and there are men who call themselves physicians who will act as helpers in this hellish business. Such a one ought not to put "M.D." after his name, but "D.M."—damnable murderer. In our country they hang them, which is just. Alas, they do not always catch them. I said this in an Australian city, and the wife of a physician was very indignant about it. But her indignation did not alter the truth of what I said. It only exposed a guilty party.

Being Faithful, Honest, and Satisfied with What You Have

The seventh command is, "Thou shalt not commit adultery." There is no class of sins upon which God has set the stamp of His disapproval in a plainer way, by the fearful consequences that immediately follow the sins covered by this commandment. The woman untrue to her husband, the husband untrue to his wife: the curse of God always follows them. It may be done by legal means, under the cover of divorce laws that controvert God's laws, but it does not lessen the sin. The meanest scoundrel that walks the earth, the meanest man alive, is the man who steps in, under any circumstances, between a man and his wife; and the meanest woman on earth is the one who steps in between another woman and her husband.

Remember, furthermore, that our Savior interpreted this law as applying not only to the overt act but to the secret thought of the heart, when He said, "Whosoever looketh on a woman to lust after her hath committed adultery with her already in his heart" (Matthew 5:28).

The eighth commandment reads, "Thou shalt not steal." How much are weighed by that law? Wait a moment. What is it to steal? To steal is to take property from another without giving an adequate equivalent in either property or money. For example, every man who sells goods under false pretenses is a thief. The man who sells a piece of cloth as being "all wool" when it is part cotton is a thief. The man who employs labor, and takes advantage of the poor man's necessity, and does not give him in pay a full equivalent for his labor, is a thief. Every laboring man who does not give to his employer, in good honest work, a fair equivalent for the wages paid to him, is a thief. The gambler who gambles and wins is a thief. Every time you bet on cards, on a horse race, on a boat race, every time you invest in pools or in a lottery, whether it be a public lottery or a church lottery, and win, you are a thief. The man who gambles and wins is a thief; the man who gambles and loses is a fool. So every gambler is either a thief or a fool.

The ninth commandment reads, "Thou shalt not bear false witness against thy neighbour." I know you do not like what I am saying, but that does not alter it; and you will not escape God by trying to forget what I say. But if you do not pay attention to my words, as far as they are true, they will rise up against you in the day of judgment.

How much do you weigh, weighed by that commandment? "Well," you say, "I am all right by that, because I was never in court." Does it say anything about court? Every time you tell anything about another that is derogatory to them, and is not true, you have broken this law of God. You hear a story, and do not take pains to find out whether it is true or not. Perhaps you add a bit to it, and go on and tell it, and it is not true. You have broken the law of God. You say, "I thought it was true." It is not what you think: it is the fact. Whenever you hear anything against a neighbor, do not believe it until it is proven absolutely to be true; and even when it is, keep it to yourself, unless duty clearly demands the telling of it, which is very seldom.

Some of you say, "Did you hear that awful story about Mrs. —? I was awfully sorry." You lie. You were glad to hear it, or you would have kept it to yourself. The gossip, the slanderer, is viler than the vilest thief who walks your streets. The thief only steals money: the slanderer steals what money cannot buy—reputation.

The tenth command tells us, "Thou shalt not covet thy neighbour's house, thou shalt not covet thy neighbour's wife, nor his manservant, nor his maidservant, nor his ox, nor his ass, nor any thing that is thy neighbour's."—God's law covers not only the overt act but the covert thought of the heart as well. Many of you would not steal your neighbor's horse, but you wish it was yours. You would not run off with your neighbor's wife, but you wish she were yours. You would not rob your neighbor of his money, but you wish it was your money. You have broken the law of God.

Two Even Greater Commandments

How much do you weigh, weighed by the law of God? There are two other weights heavier than these.

"All things whatsoever ye would that men should do to you, do ye even so to them" (Matthew 7:12). Jesus declared the so-called Golden Rule. How many talk about it, and how few keep it.

One day I was talking to a sea captain. I asked him, "Captain, why are you not a Christian?" "The Golden Rule is a good enough religion for me," he replied. "Do you keep it?" He dropped his head. He talked about it, but he did not keep it. Talking about it will not save you. Do you do it? Mind it does not merely put it negatively, "Do not do to others whatsoever ye would not that they should do to you." That is Confucianism. The Christian rule is positive. "Do these things to them." Sell goods to other people just the way you want other people to sell goods to you. Talk about other people behind their backs just as you want them to talk about you behind your back. Do you do it? Always? If not, you are weighed and found wanting.

The heaviest weight of all is in Matthew 22:37–38: "Thou shalt love the Lord thy God with all thy heart, and with all thy soul, and with all thy mind. This is the first and great commandment." How much do you weigh by that law? Put God first in everything—in business, in politics, in social life, in study, in everything. Do you do it? Have you always done it? No, you say, I have not. Then you are weighed and found wanting, not only by breaking a law of God, but this is "the first and great commandment." You have broken the first and greatest of God's laws.

A minister asked me to talk to a young man who wanted to go into the ministry. He was a splendid-looking fellow. When he came to me, and I said, "You want to go into the ministry. Are you a Christian?"

"Why, of course I am. I was brought up a Christian, and I am not going back on the training of my parents."

"Have you been born again?"

"What?"

"Jesus says, 'Except a man be born again, he cannot see the kingdom of God.'"

"Well," he said, "I have never heard of that before."

"Did you know that you had committed the greatest sin a man can commit?"

"No, I never did."

"What do you think it is?"

"Murder."

"You are greatly mistaken. Let us see what God says." I turned to Matthew 22:37–38, and read: "Thou shalt love the Lord thy God with all thy heart, and with all thy soul, and with all thy mind. This is the first and great commandment." "Which commandment is it?" I asked.

"The first and greatest."

"Have you kept it? Have you loved God with all your heart, and all your soul, and all your mind? Have you put God first in everything—in business, in pleasure, in social life, in politics?"

"No, sir, I have not. . . . I have broken the first and greatest of God's commandments. I have committed the greatest sin a man can commit. But I never saw it before."

How much do we weigh, every one of us, including the preacher? Every one of us is weighed and found wanting. What shall we do then? This is where the Gospel comes in. I have preached up to this point nothing but law. God has weighed the whole world in the balances and found it wanting, and in Christ He provided salvation for a wanting world.

God sent His Son, who kept that law, and then died for you and me who have broken it; and all you and I have to do is to take Christ into the balances with us. Christ can weigh up all the weights. When we take Christ into the balance with us, then we are weighed and found not wanting.

Will you take Jesus Christ into the balances with you tonight? Woe to the man who is weighed in the balances of God for the last time without having Jesus Christ with him. This may be the last opportunity for some; it may at all events be the last opportunity that you will ever take. The time will come when you will be weighed and found wanting; and you will look back and say, "Oh, why did I not listen to the preacher?" You will remember this sermon and the text; and you will say, "Oh, if I only had improved the opportunity."

Mr. Moody told a story I shall never forget. A man was set to watch a drawbridge. He had orders not to open the draw until a special train passed. Boat after boat came up and urged him to open the bridge and let them through. "No, I have my orders to wait till the special passes." At last a friend came up and over-urged him, and he allowed himself to be persuaded. He threw the draw open.

No sooner was the bridge well open and the vessels beginning to enter, than he heard the whistle of the special. He sprang to the lever, but he was too late. The train came on with lightning speed. He looked on as it dashed into the open chasm, he heard the shrieks of the injured and saw the corpses of the dead, and went mad. He never recovered his senses, but walked up and down the padded cell of the asylum, crying, "Oh! if I only had; oh! if I only had." Had what? Obeyed orders.

Men and women, reject Christ for the last time, and you will walk up and down the eternal madhouse, wringing your hands and saying, "Oh! if I only had; oh! if I only had!" Had what? Obeyed God and accepted His Son as your Savior. Will you do it now?

4

Every Man's Need of a Refuge

AT THE PODIUM

If "Found Wanting" brought the listener before the judgment seat of God's law and offered Christ as the only possible way of measuring up, "Every Man's Need of a Refuge" looks more widely at a host of things that threaten us and presents Christ as the shelter from them. In its unusually wide range of literary references and its appeal to personal experience, this sermon develops the subjective side of Torrey's appeal to the audience and ends, appropriately, with a direct appeal to accept Christ.

Source: From R. A. Torrey. "Every Man's Need of a Refuge." *Revival Addresses*. New York: Revell, 1903, 62–75.

I have a very precious Old Testament text tonight, Isaiah 32:2. "And a man shall be as an hiding place from the wind, and a covert from the tempest; as rivers of water in a dry place, as the shadow of a great rock in a weary land."

A good many years ago I was visiting some of the art galleries of Germany, and I saw a picture in the new art gallery in Munich that made a very deep impression on my mind. It represented the approach of a storm; the thunder clouds were rolling up thick and ominous; the trees were bending before the first approach of the oncoming tempest. Horses and cattle were scurrying across the fields in fright, and a little company of men, women, and children, with bowed forms, blanched faces, and terror depicted in every look and action, were running before the storm in search of a hiding place.

I do not suppose it was the artist's intention, but it has always seemed to me that this picture was an accurate representation of every human life. Every man and woman needs a hiding place. You say a hiding place from what? A hiding place from four things.

An Escape from an Accusing Conscience

First of all, every one of us needs *a hiding place from the accusations of our own conscience.* Every man and woman here tonight has a conscience, and every man and woman here tonight has sinned against their own conscience. There is no torment like the torment of an accusing conscience. We do not have to go to the Word of God to find that out. We find it in heathen literature as well. It was not a Christian poet but a heathen of about the time of Christ, the Latin poet Juvenal, who said:

Trust me, no torture that the poets feign
Can match the fierce, unutterable pain
He feels, who, night and day, devoid of rest,
Carries his own accuser in his breast.

It was another heathen poet, though he lived in a Christian land, the poet Lord Byron, who wrote:

Thus the dark in soul expire
Or live like scorpion, girt with fire,
Thus writhes the soul remorse hath riven,

Unfit for earth, undoomed for heaven;
Darkness above, despair beneath,
Around him gloom, within him death.[1]

But we do not need to go to the poets to find out the torments of an accusing conscience. We find them round about us every day in actual life and experience. One night at the close of a service, at the church of which I am now pastor in Chicago, there came to me a woman with a haunted face and said, "I would like to see you. In private." I replied, "If you will come to my office tomorrow at 2 p.m., I will have the pastor there; and if you have anything to say, we shall be glad to listen."

The next day at two o'clock the woman came to my office, and Mr. Hyde, the pastor, was present, and I said to the woman, "Now what is the trouble?" She made an effort to speak and failed. Again I said, "What is the trouble?" Now she made an effort, and again failed. For the third time I said, "What is the trouble? We cannot help you unless you tell us your trouble." Then she gasped out, "I have killed a man. It was fourteen years ago, across the Atlantic Ocean, in the Old Country, in the darkness of a forest, I drove a dagger into a man's throat and dropped the dagger and ran away. He was found in the forest with the dagger by his side.

"Nobody suspected me, but everybody thought he had committed suicide. I stayed there two years, and nobody ever suspected me; but I knew I had done it and was wretched, and at last I came to America to see if I could find peace here. First I went to New York and then came to Chicago, and I have been here twelve years but have not found peace. I often go to the lake and stand on the pier and look into the dark waters beneath, and I would jump in if I were not afraid of what may lie beyond death."

Haunted and hunted by her own conscience for fourteen years! Hell on earth! Well, someone says, "I can very readily see how a person who has committed so awful a deed as that, staining her hands with human blood, should be haunted by her conscience. But I have never done a thing like that." That may be, but you have sinned; and when conscience points at us the finger of accusation, we do not so much balance up the greatness or the smallness of our sin. But you say, "My conscience does not trouble me." That may be, for it is a well-known psychological fact that conscience sometimes sleeps, but conscience never dies. The day is coming when that sleeping conscience of yours will awaken, and your conscience will point at you the finger of accusation, and woe be to the man whose conscience wakes up, who has no hiding place from his own conscience.

In the city of Toronto years ago, there was a young girl who had drifted there from the country. She had heard of the gaieties of the place and had left her home and come there for a life of pleasure, going to theatres and dances and amusements of that sort, and like many another that goes to the great city with the same object, she was caught in the maelstrom of the city's sin and had gone down, down, down into a life of shame. Her conscience did not trouble her; but one night the Fiske Jubilee Singers were singing in Toronto, and some friends asked the girl to go and hear them, and she did. At last they came to that hymn with the weird refrain:

> My mother once, my mother twice,
> My mother she'll rejoice;
> In heaven once, in heaven twice,
> My mother she'll rejoice.

The poor girl was sitting up in the gallery, and as she heard the strains of that chorus floating up to her, all the memory of her childhood came back; she was a child, and at home again, in the old home. It was evening; the lamp stood upon the table, and her sweet-faced mother sat there with open Bible on her lap, and she a little girl of four, with golden hair, was kneeling at her mother's knee, learning to pray. It all came back again to her. Again the Jubilee Singers came to that refrain:

My mother once, my mother twice,
My mother she'll rejoice;
In heaven once, in heaven twice,
My mother she'll rejoice.

And as those words came floating up again, the hot blood came to the girl's cheeks, she sprang to her feet and rushed down the stairs out into the streets of the great city. On, on, on, as fast as her feet, now growing weary, could take her, out beyond the gaslights into the country; and next morning, when a certain farmer came to his farmhouse door, there was the poor girl, clutching the threshold, dead! Hunted to death by her own conscience.

Oh, there are men and women here tonight whose consciences are asleep, but whose consciences will someday awaken, and woe be to the man or woman whose conscience wakes up and who has no hiding place from it.

An Escape from the Power of Sin within Ourselves

In the second place, we need *a hiding place from the power of sin within ourselves.* Now every man and woman here tonight who know themselves at all well know that there are powers of evil resident within themselves that are more than they can master in their own strength. If there is any man or woman who thinks they have a complete mastery over themselves, if there is any man who thinks he has power to break away in his own strength from the sin that is within, he is a sadly deceived man. There are some people here tonight with the overmastering appetite for strong drink. There are others who do not care for it at all but are enslaved by other sins. Others have a passion for gambling. Others care for neither of these but have a love for other things. With another it is an ungovernable temper; with others it is a sharp, unkind, censorious tongue.

With some it is one thing and with some another. But with every man and woman of us within these four walls, there is the power of sin within ourselves, which is more than we can master in our own strength. We need a hiding place from the power of sin within.

I remember one night a young man came to me at the close of a meeting like this, in Minneapolis, and he said, "I heard you speaking in the street tonight, and I said to myself, 'that man can help me,' and I have come here and stayed through the service. Will you now help me?" I said I would be very glad to do so if I could. He said: "Listen; I was employed down in Pennsylvania, and I got to leading a fast life. Now," he said, "you know that a fast life costs money. It costs more than I earned, and I put my hand into my employer's money-till and took his money.

"Of course I was caught, but my employer was a good man. He might have sent me to prison; instead of that, he said, 'You must go to the Northwest. It is a new country; begin life anew up there.' They sent me here, and I have now got a good position, as you see by my uniform," and he pointed to it. "But," he said, "I am going just the same way in Minneapolis that I went in Pennsylvania. I am afraid to leave this hall tonight. Before I get a block from this hall, I shall meet someone who knows me, and just as sure as I do I am lost."

You may have no weakness in the direction that this young man had, and again you may have; but every man and woman here has the power of sin within that is more than they can master in their own strength. We need a hiding place from the power of sin within.

An Escape from the Power of the Devil

In the third place, we need *a hiding place from the power of the Devil.* In our country there are a great many people who are too wise to believe in the existence of a personal devil. I believe in the existence of a personal devil. I will tell you why. In the first place, because the Old Book says so, and I have found that the man who believes in the Bible always comes out ahead in the long run, and that the man who is too wise and too advanced to believe the Word of God comes out behind, in the long run, every time.

Now, there was a time when I was so wise that I believed so much of the Bible as was wise enough to agree with me. Thank God, that time has passed. Thank God, He has opened my eyes and ears until I have come to the place where I know—I wish I had time to tell you how I know—that that Book, from the first chapter to the last, is the very Word of God. Now this Book teaches us that there is a personal devil. Turn to 1 Peter 5:8: "Because your adversary the devil, as a roaring lion, walketh about, seeking whom he may devour." Ephesians 6:11–12: "Put on the whole armour of God, that ye may be able to stand against the wiles of the devil. For we wrestle not against flesh and blood, but against principalities, against powers, against the rulers of the darkness of this world, against spiritual wickedness in high places."

But friends, there is another reason why I believe in a personal devil, and that is because of the teaching of my own experience and my common sense. Years ago a great Frenchman of science was crossing the Arabian desert under the leadership of an Arab guide. When the sun was setting in the west, the guide spread his praying rug down upon the ground and began to pray. When he had finished, the man of science stood looking at him with scorn and asked him what he was doing. He said, "I am praying." "Praying! Praying to whom?" "To Allah, to God." The man of science said, "Did you ever see God?" "No." "Did you ever hear God?" "No." "Did you ever put out your hands and touch God and feel Him?" "No." "Then you are a great fool to believe in a God you never saw, a God you never heard, a God you never put out your hand and touched."

The Arab guide said nothing. They retired for the night, rose early the next morning, and a little before sunrise they went out from the tent. The man of science said to the Arab guide, "There was a camel round this tent last night."

With a peculiar look in his eye, the Arab said, "Did you see the camel?"

"No."

"Did you hear the camel?"

"No."

"Did you put out your hand and touch the camel?"

"No."

"Well, you are a strange man of science to believe in a camel you never saw, a camel you never heard, a camel you never put out your hands and touched."

"Oh, but," said the other, "here are his footprints all around the tent."

Just then the sun was rising in all its oriental splendor, and with a graceful wave of his barbaric hand, the guide said, "Behold the footprints of the Creator, and know that there is a God." I think the untutored savage had the best of the argument. Friends, we see everywhere in this magnificent universe the footprints of the Creator.

But, alas! We see everywhere in human society the footprints of the enemy. Why, you have only to walk the streets of London and you see the footprints of Satan; you see them in your dens of infamy, in the faces of the men and women on the streets, and, alas! You see the footprints of Satan in the homes of culture and refinement. What means it that men and women of education, men and women of refinement, fall under the power of all these strange delusions, of Christian Science, Theosophy, and all that sort of nonsense? It means that there is a devil—cunning, subtle, masterly, marvelous—more than a match for you and me in cunning and power. We need a hiding place from the subtlety, the cunning, the power, of the Devil.

An Escape from the Wrath to Come

In the fourth place, we need a hiding place from the wrath to come. A great many people do not believe that there is "a wrath to come." I do. Why? Again, because the Old Book says so. The Old Book says that "[God] has appointed a day in the which he will judge the world in righteousness" (Acts 17:31), and God has given assurance of this by raising Jesus Christ from the dead. The Old Book says: "There is to be a day of wrath and revelation of the righteous judgment of a holy and outraged God" (Romans 2:5). I believe this because the Bible says so.

Another reason why I believe that there is "a wrath to come" is that my common sense says so. Look, here is a man who grows rich by overreaching his neighbors, grows rich by robbing the widow and the orphan. He does it by legal means. Oh, yes, he is too cunning to come within reach of the law. But he grows rich by making other people poor. He increases in wealth and is honored and respected. When he goes down the streets in his magnificent equipage, the gentleman on the street turns and says to his son: "There goes Mr. So-and-so, a man of rare business ability, a man who is now one of our leading men of capital. I hope, my boy, when you grow up, you will be as successful as he." He lives in honor, dies in honor, dies respected by everybody—almost. And the victims of his rapacity, the victims of his oppression, the victims of his dishonesty lie yonder, bleaching in the potter's field, where they have gone prematurely because of his robbery.

Do you mean to tell me that there will not be a day when these men who have lived on wealth wrung from the poor widow and orphan will not have to go before a righteous God and answer for it, and receive what they never received in this world, the fit reward of their dishonesty? Of course there is a Judgment Day; of course there is a hell.

Look here, here is a man who goes through life, never giving God one thought from one year to another. He leaves God out of his business, leaves God out of his social life, leaves God out of his study, leaves God out of his pleasures, and makes God's day a day of pleasure, God's Book never opened, God's Son trampled underfoot. And thus the man lives, and thus he dies, going through the world, ignoring the God that made him and gave His Son to die upon the cross to save him.

Do you mean to tell me that there will not be a day when that man will have to go up before a righteous God and answer these questions: "What did you do with My day?" "What did you do with My laws?" "What did you do with My Word?" "What did you do, above all, with My Son?" Of course there is a Judgment Day. And you and I need a hiding place from it, every one of us, for every one of us has sinned and come short of the glory of God. There are then these four things from which we need a hiding place—our own conscience, the power of sin within, the power and subtlety of the Devil, and the wrath to come.

Our Hiding Place

Is there a hiding place? I read my text again: "A man shall be as an hiding place from the wind, and a covert from the tempest; as rivers of water in a dry place, as the shadow of a great rock in a weary land." "A man shall be"—who is that man? There is just one man that is a hiding place—the God-man, Jesus Christ. He is a hiding place from conscience.

I have told you part of a story, and I will now tell you the rest. When that woman came and told me how she had been haunted by her conscience for fourteen years, I took the Bible and said to her, "Do you believe what is written in this Book?"

She said, "Yes, sir, I believe it all. I was brought up in the Lutheran Church."

"All right," I said, "listen (Isaiah 53:6): 'All we like sheep have gone astray.'" I said, "Is that true of you?"

"Oh, sir," she said, "it is."

"'We have turned every one to his own way!' Is that true of you?"

"Oh, yes, that is the trouble. It is true."

"What are you?"

"I am *lost.*"

"Very well, listen to the rest of it: 'And the Lord hath laid on him the iniquity of us all.' Now," I said, "who is the *him*?"

She said, "It is Jesus Christ."

"Well, listen: 'And the Lord hath laid on *Jesus Christ* the iniquity of us all.'

"Now," I said, "let my Bible represent your sin, let my right hand represent you, and my left hand Jesus Christ." I closed the Bible and repeated the text: "All we like sheep have gone astray; we have turned every one to his own way." And I laid my Bible in my right hand and said, "Where is your sin now?"

She said, "It is on me."

"Well, listen: 'The Lord hath laid on him the iniquity of us all.'" And I laid the Bible over on the other hand. "Where is your sin now?"

She hesitated and then said, "It is on Jesus Christ."

"Right!" I said. "Is it on you any longer, then?"

It was a few moments before she spoke, and then she burst out with a cry of joy: "No, it is on Jesus Christ!" That woman, who had been haunted by her conscience for fourteen years went from my office that day with the peace of God in her heart. Is there a man or woman here haunted with the memory of the past? Christ is a hiding place and there is peace tonight for you in Him.

Christ is a hiding place from sin within. I knew a young man belonging to a good family, highly educated, with noble aspirations, but completely overmastered by sin in one of its most loathesome forms. He tried to break away, tried to be a man, but failed, and he went down, deeper and deeper and deeper, until at last he was in despair and on the verge of a suicide's grave. One awful night when despair had settled on his soul, he cried to God for Christ's sake, and Christ set him free. And never once did he fall into that sin again.

Christ is a hiding place from the power of sin. I know a man in our home country—I think I never knew a man in my life more completely in the power of Satan than he was—a man of brilliant intellectual gifts, the most remarkable orator I ever heard. And yet he had gone down, and had fallen into the power of Satan, gone down until his friends had all left him, until his wife and children were wanderers, and he was a tramp on the streets. The man had gone down so low that on one occasion I was told he threw his poor wife down on the floor (one of the noblest women who ever stood by a fallen husband), and stamped on her with his heel.

"John, you ought to be repentant," I told him.

"Well, I don't believe as you do," he said. "I do not believe in God or in your Bible."

"But," I said, "John, that does not make any difference; if you will take Jesus Christ as your Savior, He will save you, and if you do not take Him, you are lost."

A few months afterward, in another city, he went to his wretched garret and threw himself upon Christ, and Jesus Christ met him and saved him and transformed him, and today he is one of the most honored men in our land. There is no mere speculation about the religion of Jesus Christ. It is a present-day demonstrable reality. It is not merely that Christ saved people nineteen hundred years ago; He is saving them today in London.

Once more, Christ is a hiding place from the wrath to come. Now, of course, I cannot prove that from experience, for it lies in the future; but I can prove it by an argument that is unanswerable. That argument is this: the Christ who has power to save men from the power of sin now certainly has power to save them from the *consequences* of sin hereafter. Is not that a good argument? Let me add, that any religion that is not saving you from the power of sin today will not save you from the consequences of sin in eternity. There is a lot of religion in this world that is absolutely worthless. People tell you that they are Christians and that they are religious. They are saying their prayers and doing all sorts of things. I will ask you a question: "Have you got that kind of faith in Jesus Christ that is saving you from the power of sin today?" If you have, you have that kind of faith in Jesus Christ that will save you from the consequences of sin hereafter. But if you have that kind of faith in Jesus Christ—which after all is not faith, which is not saving you *now*—you have that kind of faith in Jesus Christ that won't save you from the penalty of sin hereafter.

Friends, Jesus Christ is a refuge, a hiding place from conscience and its accusations, from the power of sin within, from the power of Satan, from the wrath to come, from all that man needs a hiding place from. Who will come to this hiding place tonight?

Note

1. George Byron, "The Giaour," a narrative poem published in 1813.

5

Refuges of Lies

AT THE PODIUM

In *How to Bring Men to Christ*, the how-to book in which Torrey described how different kinds of people respond to hearing the gospel, he gave much attention to the category of the hearer who deludes himself with false comfort. In this sermon, taken from *Revival Addresses*, Torrey confronts such listeners directly, challenging their false hopes with a series of searching questions.

Source: R. A. Torrey. "Refuges of Lies." *Revival Addresses*. New York: Revell, 1903, 112–29.

We have seen in a former address that every man needs a refuge from four things—from the accusations of his own conscience, from the power of sin within, from the power of Satan, and from the wrath to come. Almost every man has a refuge, that is, he has something in which he has put his trust to comfort him. The difficulty with most men is not so much that they have not a refuge, as that they have a false refuge, a refuge that will fail them in the hour of crisis and need; what our text, Isaiah 28:17, characterizes as a "refuge of lies."

It was just so in Isaiah's time; the men of Israel knew there was a coming day of judgment, and that they needed a hiding place from that coming judgment of God, and they made lies their refuge, and Isaiah—God's messenger—proclaimed, "the hail shall sweep away [your false refuge] the refuge of lies," and I come to you with the same message, you men and women that have a refuge, but a false one: "The hail shall sweep away the refuge of lies."

Five Tests to Reveal a Refuge of Lies

Is there any way in which we can tell a true refuge from a false one, a refuge that will stand the test of the coming day of God from a refuge that the hail will sweep away? There are five tests that will commend themselves to the reason and common sense of every intelligent and candid man here tonight, whereby he can tell a true refuge from a false one, a refuge that will save from a refuge that will ruin; a refuge of truth from a refuge of lies.

The first test is this: *A true refuge is one that meets the highest demands of your own conscience.* If that in which you are trusting does not meet the highest demands of your own conscience, it certainly is not a hiding place from the accusations of conscience. Furthermore, it is not a hiding place from the wrath of God, for if our own hearts condemn us, God is greater than our heart, and knows all things.

The second test is this: *Every true refuge is one that is making you a better man or woman today.* If you are trusting in something that is not making you a better man or woman today, it is not a hiding place from the power of sin within, it is not a hiding place from the power of Satan, it is not a hiding place from the wrath to come; for a refuge that does not save you from the power of sin here on earth, very certainly will never save you from the consequences of sin hereafter.

The third test is this: *A true refuge is one that will stand the test of the dying hour.* If you are trusting in something that simply brings you comfort when you are well and strong, but will fail you in that great hour that we have all got to face, when we lie face-to-face with death and eternity, it is absolutely worthless.

The fourth test is this: *A true refuge is one that will stand the test of the Judgment Day*. If you are trusting in something that will not stand the test of that great Judgment Day, when we have to pass before the judgment bar of God to give an account of the deeds done in the body, it is absolutely worthless.

There are men here in London indicted for murders and about to be tried. Now suppose you went down to see one of these men, and you found him in a very peaceful frame of mind, without a fear, and you said to him, "Well, you seem very cheerful for a man charged with murder."

"Oh, yes," he says, "I am; I have no anxiety whatever about that trial."

"What, no anxiety about it?"

"No, none whatever," he replies.

"Why not?"

"Because," says he, "I have an answer to make."

"Well, is your answer one that will satisfy the judge and jury?" you ask.

"No," he replies, "I do not think it will satisfy the judge and jury, but it satisfies me."

"Why?" you would say. "What good is it if your answer satisfies you, if it will not satisfy the judge and jury before whom the case is to be tried." The question is not whether your hope satisfies you; will it satisfy God?

I might add a fifth test: Will it stand the test of the Word of God? This is the supreme test, though in what follows I will not always raise this question. Our four tests are enough to expose any refuge.

Here then are the four tests: first, Is it meeting the highest demands of your own conscience? Second, Is it making you a better man or woman? Third, Will it stand the test of the dying hour? Fourth, Will it stand the test of the Judgment Day?

The False Refuge of Morality

Now we are going to apply these four tests to the things in which men are trusting.

The first is they trust *their own conscience.* How many men in London there are, who, if you go up and speak with them, and ask them to come to Christ, say, "No, I will not come; I do not need Him." You ask, "Why not?" And they reply, "Because I am a good man; my life and character are such that I do not feel the need of a Savior, and I am trusting in my life and character to gain acceptance before God."

Let us apply the four tests. You are trusting in your own goodness. Does your own goodness meet the highest demands of your own conscience? Is there a person here tonight who will say, "My life and character are such that they meet the highest demands of my own conscience"? Is there a man out of Christ here tonight who will say that? I have never met but two men who have said it. "They must have been remarkably good men," you will say. No, they had remarkably poor consciences.

The first one was a man I once met while crossing the Atlantic Ocean. I approached him on the subject of becoming a Christian. He said, "I do not need any Savior." I said, "Do you mean to tell me your life has been such, and your character from childhood up to this moment, as to satisfy the highest demands of your own conscience?" He said, "Yes, they have." But so far from being an exceptionally good man, he was the most unpopular man on the boat before we reached New York City.

Now the second test. Is *trust in your goodness* making you a better person? As you go on from month to month and from year to year, do you find that you are growing more kind, more gentle, more self-sacrificing, more thoughtful of others, more considerate, more tender, more humble, more prayerful? Now I have known a great many men who trusted in their own goodness but I have yet to meet the first one who, while trusting to his own goodness, grew better. As far as my experience goes, these men grow hard, grow censorious, grow harsh, grow selfish, grow more and more inconsiderate of others, grow more proud, and more bitter.

Third, will morality stand *the test of the dying hour*? Oh, how many a man has gone through life boasting of his morality, and trusting in his morality to save him in the life to come; but when that dread hour comes, when he lies upon his dying bed face-to-face with God and eternity, all his trust in his morality leaves him, in that illumination that comes to the soul as eternity draws nigh. I remember a man in one of my pastorates who was very, very self-confident. He had no use for the church, no use for the Bible, no use for Jesus Christ. He was very well satisfied that he was about the most exemplary man there was in the community, and he needed no Savior. But the time came when there was a cancer eating into that man's brain. It was eating through the skin, eating through the flesh, it was eating into the skull, and eating so far into the skull that there was only a thin film left.

When that man saw that he had but a few days, and possibly but a few hours, to live, his trust in his morality fled, and he said, "I wish you would go and call Mr. Torrey to come here and see me." I came to the bedside, and as he lay there in agony he said to me, "Tell me what to do to be saved." I sat down by that bed and tried to show him from the Word of God what he must do to be saved. And as night came on I said to his family, "Do not sit up through the long hours of the night; I will stay up with him and perform all that is necessary." And all through the hours of the night, I sat beside that dying man's bed. Sometimes I had to go out of the room to get something for him, and whenever I came back there was always one groan from the bed over in the corner. It was this: "Oh, I wish I was a Christian! I wish I was a Christian! I wish I was a Christian!" And so he died. His morality did not stand the test of the dying hour.

Fourth, will your morality stand the *test of the Judgment Day*, when you stand face-to-face with an infinitely holy God who knows you through and through? Will you look up into His face and say, "O God, I stand here on my merits, on my character and life! Thou knowest my life; Thou knowest me through and through; Thou knowest my every secret thought and act; Thou knowest my life is pure, and I stand here before an infinitely holy God, and am proud of my morality."

The fifth question is, *Will it stand the test of God's Word*? Turn to Romans 3:20: "Therefore by the deeds of the law there shall no flesh be justified in his sight." Turn to Galatians 3:10: "For as many as are of the works of the law are under the curse: for it is written, Cursed is every one that continueth not in all things which are written in the book of the law to do them."

The False Refuge of Other People's Badness

There is a second refuge of lies, and that is, *trust in other people's badness.* Some men trust in their own goodness; other men trust in other folks' badness. You go to them and talk about Christ, and they say, "Well, I am just as good as other folks. I am just as good as a lot of your professing Christians." Oh, I know so many hypocrites in the church. Instead of making their boast of, and putting their trust in, their own goodness, they make a boast of, and put their trust in, other people's badness.

Let us apply the tests. *Does that mean the highest demands of your conscience*? When your conscience comes to you with its lofty demands, does it satisfy your conscience to say, "Well, I am just as good as a great many professing Christians"? If it does, you have a conscience of a very low order. Is trust in other people's badness making you a better man? Now, I have known a good many people, just as you have known them, who were all the time talking about the badness of other people. I have yet to meet the first one that grew better by the process.

Show me the man or woman who is all the time dwelling upon

the badness of other people, and I will show you a man or woman who is bad themselves, every time. Show me the man that is always talking about another man's adultery, and you show me a man who is an adulterer himself. Show me the woman that is always having a suspicion about other women, and I will show you a woman you cannot trust. Show me a man who says every other man is dishonest, and I will show you a man who is a knave himself.

I once had a Bible class, and in that class there was a woman who was in business, one of those women who was always talking about the faults of others; and one day this woman propounded this question to me; she said: "Mr. Torrey, is it not true that every person in business is dishonest?" I looked at her and said, "When any person in business comes to me and asks if everyone in business is not dishonest, they convict at least one person." She was angry, but I was only telling her the truth. Show me the man or woman who is always dwelling upon the faults of Christians, or the faults of anybody else, and I will show you a man or woman who is rotten to the core. I made that remark in my church when I was pastor in an American city, and at the close of the meeting, a lady came and said to me, "I do not like what you said; you said, 'If you show me any man or woman that is always talking about the faults of others, you would show me someone that was bad.'"

"Yes," I said, "and I mean it."

"Well, there is Miss So-and-so. Now you must admit that she is always talking about the faults of others." I had to admit that this was a well-known fact. "You do not mean to say that she is bad herself?"

I did not answer, for I did not care to be personal; but if I had told her all the truth, I would have told her that that very week I had forbidden that very woman to sing in the choir anymore because of certain revelations of her character that had been made to me, and to which she had confessed.

Will it stand the test of the dying hour? When you come to lie on your dying bed, will it give all the comfort you need to be thinking about the faults of others? No. This very woman who accused every person in business of being dishonest, who was always dwelling upon the faults of others—the time came for her to die; and as she lay dying, the doctor came in and said: "Mrs. So-and-so, it is my duty to tell you that you must die." The woman shrieked, "I cannot die; I won't die; I am not ready to die"; but she did die.

Will it stand the test of the Judgment Day? When you go into the presence of God to answer to Him, will you look up into His face with the same confidence as you look up into mine, and say, "O God, I do not pretend to have been very good, but I was just as good as a great many in the churches"? Will you do it, man? Will you do it, woman? Ah, the blessed Book tells you, in Romans 14:12: "So then every one of us shall give an account of himself to God." Not an account of somebody else. In the Judgment Day you will forget everybody but yourself. In that Judgment Day all other sin will vanish but your sin.

The False Refuge of Universalism

The third refuge of lies is universalism. There are a great many men in every city, who, if you approach them on the subject of becoming Christians and giving up sin, say, "Oh, no, I will not do that; I believe in a God of love; I believe God is too good to damn anybody. A man does not need to forsake sin in order to take Christ. God is good, and there is not any hell. Do you mean to tell me God would permit a hell; that a good God would damn anyone? No, I do not need to forsake sin. I am trusting in the goodness of God, and I believe all men will at some time or other be saved."

Now, let us just try this. Does that meet the highest demands of conscience? When your conscience comes to you and points out your sin and demands your renunciation, does it satisfy your conscience to say, "Yes, I am doing wrong, but God is so good I can just as well go on sinning, I can just as well go on trampling God's laws underfoot. He is so good He will not punish me. He gave His Son to die for me; I can go on sinning as I please"?

Does that satisfy your conscience? Well, then, you have a mighty mean conscience. What would you think of a boy and girl, brother and sister, whose mother lies sick in the house. The boy was sick a little time before, and the mother had watched over him so faithfully and tenderly that she had caught his sickness; she had brought him back to health, but she was lying very sick and almost at the point of death. She had told the children that they could go out into the garden and said, "There are some flowers out there about which I am very careful. I do not want you to pick them." So Johnny and Mary go out, and Johnny goes to work to do just what he was asked not to do. His sister expostulates and says, "Johnny, did you not hear mother tell us not to pick those flowers, that they were very precious and that she did not want them picked?" "Oh, yes," says Johnny. "Then why pick them?" asks the sister. "Because," says Johnny, "she loves me so, Mary. Don't you know how she loves me, how when I was sick mother gave up sleep and everything, and watched over me through the nights? Don't you know that she is sick there now because she loves me so? And so I am now going to do the very thing she told me not to do."

What would you think of a boy like that, and what do you think of the man or woman who makes their boast of the love of God, and because God loves them with such a wonderful love, make His love an excuse for sin, make God's love an excuse for rebellion against Him, make God's love a reason for a worldly and careless life? I should think you men and women would despise yourselves. Oh, the baseness of it; oh, the contemptible ingratitude of it; oh, the black-heartedness of it, making God's wondrous love, that gave Jesus to die on the cross of Calvary, an excuse for sinning against Him!

Is your universalism making you a better man or woman? Oh, how many men grow careless, grow worldly, grow sinful, grow indifferent, because somebody has inoculated them with the pernicious error of eternal hope. How many men there are alive now, once earnest in the service of God, who are indifferent about the condition of the lost, the worldly, and the careless, because they have read some books undermining, or trying to undermine, the doctrines of Jesus and the apostles. With what honeyed words the professing church today is promulgating the doctrine of eternal hope, which is an infernal lie.

Will universalism stand the test of the dying hour? Oftentimes it does not. Dr. Ichabod Spencer, one of the most able and faithful pastors America ever had, tells how, when pastor of a Presbyterian church in Brooklyn, he was called to see a young man who was dying. His wife and mother were members of the church, but this young man was not. The doctor went to see him and tried to lead him to Christ; but he turned and said, "It is no use; I have had many chances, but I have put them all away and I am dying, and shall soon have to go; it is no use talking to me now." And he was in great agony and distress of soul. Then the father came in and heard him talking and groaning, and he said, "My boy, there is no reason for you to take on so. There is no reason for you to feel so bad. You have not been a bad man; you have nothing to fear." The dying young man turned round and said to his father, "You are to blame for me being here. If I had listened to mother when she tried to lead me to a good life, instead of listening to you, I should not be in this strait. Mother tried to get me to go to Sunday school and to church, but you said God was so good it did not matter; and when Mother tried to take me to church, you took me fishing and hunting and pleasuring; you told me there was not a hell, and I believed you; you have deceived me up to this moment, Father, but you can't deceive me any longer. I am dying and I am going to hell, and my blood is on your soul." Then he turned his face to the wall and died.

Men, you turn people into sin by preaching a doctrine that contradicts the teaching of the Son of God. It means that you are deceiving the men you are rocking to sleep in sin, and they will live to curse you some day. And you men who are in health and strength are building upon a false hope. Death will tear away the veil that blinds your eyes tonight.

Will trust in universalism stand the test of the Judgment Day? When you go up into the presence of God, will you look up, and when He asks about your sin, will you answer, "Yes, Father, I did sin; I did trample Thy laws underfoot; I did neglect prayer, neglect the Bible, neglect the house of God, neglect obedience to Thee; I was worldly and careless, but I have a good answer. Father, my answer is this: I knew Thou wert a God of love, and gave Thy Son to die for me on the cross of Calvary, and as I knew Thou wert so loving, I just went on trampling Thy laws underfoot"? Will you do that? It won't stand the test.

The False Refuge of Infidelity

A fourth refuge is infidelity. How many men and women there are, who, when asked to become Christians, turn and say, "I do not believe that the Bible is the Word of God. That is an old superstition that is worn out. I do not believe that Jesus of Nazareth was the Son of God. In fact, I am not quite sure that there is a God. I am not a Christian, and you can call me what you like. Call me an infidel, an agnostic, what you please; but I do not need any Christ and do not believe in Him." He tries to comfort himself with infidelity. Hundreds of thousands are doing this in London tonight.

Apply the tests. Does that meet the highest demands of your own conscience? When conscience asserts itself and comes to you with its majestic demands, does it satisfy your conscience to say, "I do not believe in the Bible or in Jesus Christ; I do not believe in God"? Is your infidelity making you a better man? I have yet to find the first man or woman made better by infidelity. I have known men and women to be made adulterers by infidelity; I have known men to be made suicides or to be robbed of business integrity by infidelity; I have known men who were made deceivers by infidelity and ran away from their wives and went with other women. I could stand here by the hour and tell you of the characters I have known to be shipwrecked by infidelity. I have yet to find the first man that was made upright or moral or clean by infidelity.

I stood up one night in my church in Chicago. The church was full, and a great many infidels were there. I had invited them to be there, as I was talking about "Infidelity: Its Causes, Consequences, and Cure." I stopped in my sermon and said, "I want every man in this audience tonight who can honestly testify before God and this audience that he has been saved from drunkenness by the Gospel of Jesus Christ to stand up"; and two or three hundred men stood up as having been saved from drunkenness by the Gospel of Christ.

I said, "That will do. Now we are going to be fair and give the other side a chance, and I want to ask any infidel in this audience tonight that has been saved from drunkenness by infidelity in any form to stand up." I looked round; at first I thought there wasn't any one standing up. At last, away under the gallery, I saw one, a very ragged-looking sort, and he was drunk at the time; that is an actual fact. Thank God, he went down into the inquiry room afterward and thought it over. Men and women, infidelity undermines character, infidelity robs men and women of purity, infidelity makes your clerks and cashiers unsafe. You know it.

Will your infidelity stand the test of the dying hour? A great deal of infidelity does not. A friend of mine who took part in the American Civil War and fought for the North told me a story about a man in his regiment who had been boasting in camp of his unbelief. On the second day of the battle of Pittsburg Landing this man said to his comrades of his company, while waiting for the word of command to go forward, "I fear I am going to be shot this day; I have an awful feeling."

"Oh, that's nonsense," they said, "it's just a premonition, a superstition, and there's nothing in it."

Soon the command came, "Forward," and that company

marched up the hill, and just as it went over the crest, there was a volley from the enemy's guns. The first one sent a bullet through his chest near his heart, and he fell back, and as they carried him to the rear, he cried, "O God, give me time to repent!" It took only one bullet to take the infidelity out of him. It would take less than that to take the infidelity out of most of you here tonight.

Will it stand the test of the Judgment Day? Will you go up into God's presence, and when asked to answer for your sin, will you say: "Well, oh God, You know I did not quite believe You existed; I did not believe the Bible was Your Word, and that Jesus Christ was Your Son. I was an infidel; that is my answer"?

Will you do this? I will tell you how to try it. Go home tonight, and go down on your knees, and look up into God's face, and tell Him you are an infidel, and that you do not believe in Him, or in His Son, or in the Bible, and that you are willing to stand the judgment test.

I went down in a meeting like this one night to the last row of seats at the back of the hall, and I said to a man there, "Are you a Christian?"

"I should think not," he said; "I am an infidel."

I said, "Do you mean to tell me you do not believe Jesus Christ is divine?"

"No, I do not."

"Just kneel down here and tell God that," I said. He turned pale.

And I say to you tonight who profess to be infidels, "Go and tell that to God alone, not when you are trying to brave it out in the presence of others but alone; meet God alone. Get down before Him, and tell Him what you tell me."

The False Refuge of Religion

There is one more refuge of lies—*religion.* Religion is a refuge of lies. Religion never saved anybody. Trust in religion is one thing; trust in the personal Christ is another thing. Many trust in his religion, and yet they are not saved. They say, "Yes, I am religious; I go to church every Sunday; I read my prayer book and say prayers regularly every day; I read my Bible; I have been baptized; I have been confirmed or united to the church; I have taken the Sacrament regularly, and that is what I am trusting in."

Is it? Then you are lost. Let us apply the tests. Does your religion satisfy the highest demands of your conscience? Does it satisfy your conscience, when it points out your sin, to say, "I go to church; I read the Bible; I have been baptized and confirmed"? Does it really give your conscience peace? Is your religion making you a better man or woman? There is a great deal that is called religion that does not make men and women better. There is many a man who is very religious and goes to mass or to church every Sunday in the year; he goes to Confession very frequently, says his prayers regularly, reads his Bible, and partakes of Communion; he has been baptized, he has been confirmed, and yet he is just as dishonest as any other man in the community. There is many a man who is very religious, and yet oppresses his employees in the matter of wages, or robs his servants in his home. Many a most religious man is a perfect knave. Such religion will not save him but damn him with a deeper damnation.

Thirdly, will it stand the test of the dying hour? There is a great deal of religion that does not. How many people have been very religious, and yet when they come to die they tremble with fear.

Will it stand the test of the Judgment Day? Jesus Christ says it will not. In Matthew 7:22, we read: "Many will say to me in that day, Lord, Lord, have we not prophesied in thy name? and in thy name have cast out devils? and in thy name done many wonderful works?"—that is, they have been very religious; and Jesus says, "And then will I profess unto them, I never knew you: depart from me, ye that work iniquity" (v. 23). Friends, if you have nothing to trust in but religion, you are lost; it is a refuge of lies.

Well, then, is there any refuge? There is. The verse before my text gives it, Isaiah 28:16: "Therefore thus saith the Lord God, Behold, I lay in Zion for a foundation a stone, a tried stone, a precious corner stone, a sure foundation." That foundation stone is Jesus Christ. "Other foundation can no man lay than that is laid, *which is* Jesus Christ" (1 Corinthians 3:11). As I said before, it is one thing to trust in religion, and it is an entirely different thing to trust in Christ. Oh, friends, if your trust is in Christ, it will stand the test, it will meet the highest demands of your conscience. When my conscience accuses me of sin, I say—

> Jesus paid [my debt],
> All to Him I owe;
> Sin had left a crimson stain,
> He washed it white as snow.[1]

"He who had no sin was made sin for me, that I might be made the righteousness of God in Him. He Himself bore my sin in His own body on the cross"; and that satisfies the conscience. The blood of Jesus Christ gives the guilty conscience peace. Trust in Jesus Christ makes me a better man. It has completely transformed my life, my outward life and my inward life. It will stand the test of the dying hour.

Oh, how often I have gone to the room of the dying man who was trusting in Jesus, and he has looked up into my face with radiant confidence, without a tremor of fear, trusting in Jesus. I remember one day I was told that one of the former members of my Bible class was dying, and I went to his house. I walked in and he sat there propped up in bed. He was dying very fast. I said, "Mr. Pomeroy, they tell me you probably cannot live through the night."

"No," he said; "I suppose this day is my last."

I said, "Are you afraid?"

He said, with a smile of perfect peace, "Not at all."

"Mr. Pomeroy, are you ready to go?"

"I shall be glad to depart and be with Jesus Christ," he said.

When Mr. Moody was facing the other world, there was no fear. At six o'clock in the morning, his son was by his bedside and heard him whisper, "Earth is receding; heaven is opening; God is calling." Then later, "Is this death? This is not bad, this is bliss, this is glorious."

Still later, someone began to cry to God to raise him from his bed of sickness, and he said, "No, do not ask that. This is my coronation day; I have long been looking forward to it. Don't call me back; God is calling me."

Oh, friends, a living faith in Jesus Christ, the crucified and risen Savior, will stand the test of the dying hour. It will stand the test of the Judgment Day. If it is the will of God, I am ready to go and meet Him at the judgment bar tonight, and, when He asks me to answer, I have but, the all-sufficient answer, "Jesus." That will satisfy God.

Throw away your refuges of lies tonight. The hail will soon come and sweep them away; "the hail shall sweep away the refuge of lies" (Isaiah 28:17). Throw them away tonight. Take the only sure and true refuge, Jesus Christ.

Note

1. Elvina M. Hall, "Jesus Paid It All," *Worship and Service Hymnal*, 59. In public domain.

6

Three Fires

AT THE PODIUM

Torrey's sermons are punctuated with stories, but a majority of those stories are simply Torrey telling the audience what he told another audience on another occasion. That is, Torrey switches from proclamation to storytelling, but the story he tells is usually the story of how he proclaimed truth at another time. Similarly, this classic sermon, "Three Fires," begins with the story of how the idea for the sermon came to him. It is also an example of Torrey working with multiple scriptural texts in one sermon, connected by the imagery of fire.

Source: R. A. Torrey. "Three Fires." *Revival Addresses*. New York: Revell, 1903, 253–71.

One night, years ago, I was sitting at my desk in my study late at night. There was a great deal of confusion about my study table, for I had just moved that day, and had not had time to rearrange my papers. The work of the day being done, I fell into a reverie, and as I came out of that reverie I found myself gently waving back and forth in my right hand a little four-page leaflet. I do not know how it got into my hand. I suppose I took it off the table; but I don't even know how it got onto the table, for I had never seen it before.

I looked at that leaflet, and I noticed these words across the top of the leaflet in large print, "Wanted, a Baptism with Fire." It immediately fastened my attention. I said, "That is precisely what I do want; if there is anybody on this earth that needs fire, it is I," for I was born, and had grown up cold as an iceberg. So I read the leaflet. There was not much in the leaflet that impressed me, except one text, "He shall baptize you with the Holy Ghost, and with fire" (Matthew 3:11); and that not only impressed me, it kept ringing in my mind and heart, by day and by night. I could not get away from it: "He shall baptize you with the Holy Ghost, and with fire."

The following Saturday evening, when I went to a little gathering for prayer held at my church, I said to the janitor of the church, when the prayer meeting was over, "The promise says, 'He shall baptize you with the Holy Ghost, and with fire.'" A sweet smile passed over the janitor's face, and there was something about his look that made me think, "Well, the janitor seems to know all about it. I wonder if he has got something his pastor has not got."

During the days of the next week, when I sat down in my study, when I walked the streets, that kept ringing in my ears: "He shall baptize you with the Holy Ghost, and with fire." Thursday night came, and at the close of my day's work, I knelt down before God and asked Him for a text or for a subject for Sunday evening's sermon. A brother from London was going to preach for me in the morning. The only text I could see in the whole Bible was, "He shall baptize you with the Holy Ghost, and with fire," and I said, "Father, I am not to preach on Sunday morning; that is a Sunday morning text, and I don't preach in the morning. Mr. Inglis is going to preach then." I generally preach in the morning to Christians, and to the unsaved in the evening. "I want an evening text." But I could not see anything but just that one text: "He shall baptize you with the Holy Ghost, and with fire."

"Well," I said, "Father, if that is the text You want me to preach on evening or morning, I will preach on it; but I want to know." Just then there came looming up out of the Bible two other texts, and both of these texts had "fire" in them; and while I was on my knees God just opened the three texts, and I had my sermon.

The next Sunday night I went to my church and preached that sermon. When I had finished it I said, "Now all the friends who want to be baptized with the Holy Ghost and fire tonight, and all who want to be saved, come downstairs." The rooms downstairs were jammed, and when all who replied to the invitation had found room, I asked all who wanted to be baptized with the Holy Ghost and fire to go into the kindergarten room, and those who wished to be saved to go into another room, the inquiry room, and the rest to stay where they were. They began to go into both rooms; I went into the kindergarten room, where the people were sitting in the little bits of kindergarten chairs, and so closely packed that I literally had to step over their heads to get to the platform. Oh, what a time we had in that room that night!

When I came out I asked my assistant, who was in charge of the inquiry room, what sort of a time he had had, and he said, "The Spirit of God was there; and many people came out into the light." I asked Professor Towner, the choirmaster, who was left in charge of the third meeting, composed of those who had not entered either of the two rooms, and he said, "We had no meeting at all; I could not say a word; the people got right down on their knees before God, and talked to Him." I hope God will bless the Word the same way tonight. I believe He will.

The Baptism with Fire:
1. It Reveals

You will find the first of the three fires in Matthew 3:11: "I indeed baptize you with water unto repentance: but he that cometh after me is mightier than I, whose shoes I am not worthy to bear: he shall baptize you with the Holy Ghost, and with fire." That is the first of the three fires, the baptism with fire. What does it mean?

Now we know what it means to be baptized with water—we have seen that—but what does it mean to be baptized with fire? You will get your answer by asking two things: First, what is fire said to do in the Bible and, second, what happened to the apostles at Pentecost when they were baptized with the Holy Ghost and fire?

The first thing that the Bible says that fire does is, *fire reveals*. In 1 Corinthians 3:13, we read: "Every man's work shall be made manifest: for the day shall declare it, because it shall be revealed by fire." And the first thing that a baptism with fire does is to reveal what a man really is, to show us to ourselves as God sees us.

I remember the night before I preached that sermon, late on Saturday night after the sermon was all arranged, I got down and said, "Heavenly Father, I think I have a sermon for tomorrow night, but I don't believe I have got that of which the sermon speaks. I am going to preach on the baptism with the Holy Ghost and fire, and how can I preach on it if I have not had it? Now, in order that I may preach an honest sermon, baptize me with fire right now."

God heard the prayer, and the first thing that came to pass was that I had such a revelation of myself as I never had before in all my life. I had never dreamed that there was so much pride, so much vanity, so much personal ambition, so much downright meanness in my heart and life as I saw that night. And men and women, if you get a baptism with fire, I believe one of the first things that comes to you will be a revelation of yourself as God sees you. Is not that just what we need—a revelation of ourselves today that will spare us the awful humiliation of the revelation of self in that day when we stand before the judgment seat of Christ?

2. Fire Refines

The second thing that fire does is, *fire refines, or purifies*. In Malachi 3:1–3, we are told of the purifying power of fire. There is nothing that purifies like fire. Water will not cleanse as fire does. Suppose I have a piece of gold, and there is some filth on the outside of it; how can I get it off? I can wash it off with water. But suppose the filth is inside it, how will you get it out? There is only one way: throw it into the fire. Men and women, if the filth is on the outside, it can be washed away with the water of the Word; but the trouble is that the filth is on the inside, and what we need is the fire of the Holy Ghost penetrating into the innermost depths of our being, burning, burning, burning, cleansing.

What a refining came to the apostles on the day of Pentecost! How full of self-seeking they had been up to the very last supper! At the Last Supper, they had a dispute as to who should be the first in the kingdom of heaven, but after Pentecost they no longer thought of self but of Christ. How weak and cowardly they had been right up to the crucifixion! They all forsook Him and fled, and Peter denied Him at the accusation of a servant maid, with oaths and curses. But after the day of Pentecost, that same Peter who had cursed and swore and denied Christ when the servant maid accused him of being a follower of Jesus faced the very council that condemned Him, and said, "If we this day be examined of the good deed done to the impotent man, by what means he is made whole; Be it known unto you all, and to all the people of Israel, that by the name of Jesus Christ of Nazareth, whom ye crucified, whom God raised from the dead, even by him doth this man stand here before you whole" (Acts 4:9–10).

Ah, friends, cleansing is a very slow process by ordinary methods, but a baptism with fire does marvels in a moment.

3. Fire Consumes

Third, the Bible teaches us that *fire consumes*. In Ezekiel 24: 11–13 we are told of the consuming power of fire, the fire of judgment that will consume the filth and dross of Jerusalem. And the baptism of fire consumes, in fact it cleanses by consuming; it burns up all dross, all vanity, all self-righteousness, all personal ambition, all ungovernable temper.

We had once at the Bible Institute in Chicago a young woman who was much that a Christian should not be. When we heard she was coming, all of us in authority thought she never ought to have come to the Bible Institute. I thought so when I heard she was coming, for I had known her in the school from which she came, and I knew she was one of the most unmanageable scholars they ever had in the school. She was stubborn, willful, proud, quick-tempered, boisterous, loud, and pretty much everything a girl ought not to be. When I heard she was coming to the Bible Institute, I said, "So-and-so is coming to the Bible Institute! What in the world does she want at the Bible Institute?" But her uncle was one of the best friends the institute ever had, and so, out of consideration for her uncle, we admitted her.

Now, we require of every student in that Bible Institute that some definite work to save the lost should go hand in hand with Bible study; for Bible study, unless it is accompanied with actual work for the salvation of souls, will dry up a man's soul quicker than almost anything else. We required the young woman to go into the tenements, the homes of the poor and the outcast. One afternoon this girl had been visiting in Milton Avenue and Townsend Street, two of the poorest streets of Chicago. After a time she became very tired with climbing up and down the stairs, and going in and out of the filthy homes; and instead of returning to the Institute, she walked on in a very rebellious frame of mind and went down to the Lake Shore Drive, the finest avenue in Chicago, along the shore of the lake.

As she passed by those magnificent mansions there, she looked up at them with an eye that danced with pleasure, and said, "This is what I like. I have had enough of Milton Avenue; I have had enough of climbing stairs and going into tenements. This is what I like, and this is what I am going to have." She came back to the institute and went straight to her room, still in a very bitter and rebellious frame of mind. The tea-bell rang before the battle was over, and she went to the table and took her place and sat down—and there at the tea table the fire of God fell right where that girl was sitting. She sprang from her seat and rushed over to a friend at another table, and threw her arms around her and exclaimed, "I am a volunteer for Africa!" and the fire of God in a moment burned, and burned, and burned, until that young woman was so changed, her actions were so changed—her views of life, her tastes, her ambitions, her very face was so changed in a moment—that when her old friends saw her, and heard her they could hardly believe their own eyes and ears.

Later she went back to that same school down in Massachusetts, where she had been such a hindrance, and with burning words poured out her heart to the girls there, and with mighty power led them to the Lamb of God who takes away the sins of the world.

Is not that what we need tonight, a fire that will burn up this pride of ours, this selfishness of ours, this vanity of ours, this worldliness of ours, burn up all these things that hinder the world from coming to Christ, because we make men think that Christianity is unreal? You women with unconverted husbands, is not that what you need, a baptism with fire, transforming your life and clothing it with beauty, so that your husbands will say, "I must have what my wife has got"?

4. Fire Illuminates

Fourth, *fire illuminates.* Often when in Chicago I look off toward the northwest of the city. Suddenly I see the heavens lit up and then grow dark again, then they are illuminated once more and then darkened. The great foundry doors had been opened and shut, and opened and shut, and this light in the heavens was the glow from the furnaces.

Fire illuminates, but no fire illuminates like "the baptism with the Holy Ghost, and fire." When a man is baptized with the Holy Ghost and fire, truth that was dark to him before becomes instantly as bright as day; passages in the Bible that he could not understand before become as simple as A, B, C, and every page of God's Holy Word glows with heavenly light.

A baptism with fire will do more to take the infidelity and skepticism and false doctrine out of a man than any university education. How many a young fellow comes out of a theological education more than half an infidel, but the great day comes when that half-infidel preacher is baptized with the Holy Ghost and fire, and his doubts and his questionings and his criticisms go to the winds. How many an untaught or half-taught man has so wonderful an acquaintance with the truth of God that men who are scholars sit at his feet with profound astonishment, because he has been illuminated with the baptism with the Holy Ghost and fire!

Take the case of this girl again. I was away when the event I described happened, and the first thing I heard when I returned was what had taken place with her. I was going from the men's side of the institute, and was passing between the church and the women's department when this young girl turned into the gate and met me. She looked up into my face and said, "Oh, Professor Torrey, have you heard?"

"Yes, Jack, I have heard," I said, and, by the way, that is an indication of her character that she should be called Jack. "I have heard what has happened," I told her, and then she just began to pour out her soul. She fairly danced on the sidewalk as she told me, and I knew for once what it meant to dance before the Lord! Then she closed this way: "One of the best things about it is that the Bible is a new book. The Bible used to be just the stupidest book I ever read, and I didn't believe it was the Word of God at all. I did believe in the divinity of Jesus Christ, because your lectures compelled me. But the Bible was a stupid book. But oh, now God is showing me such wonderful things in the Bible."

Now, be honest. Are there not some of you tonight who profess to be Christians, to whom the Bible is a stupid book? If you would tell the honest truth, would you not rather read a novel than the Bible? You do read the Bible, because you think you ought to, but you get no enjoyment out of it. What you need is a baptism with the Holy Ghost and fire, and that would make the Bible a new book; glory would shine from every page.

5. Fire Makes Things Warm and Glowing

The next thing that fire does is, *fire makes warm, it makes to glow*. You stand before a furnace door, behind which is a glowing fire. You have in your hand a bar of iron; it is cold, and black, and forbidding, and there is no beauty in it. But you take that cold, dark, forbidding bar of iron, and you open the furnace door and thrust it into the glowing fire. Soon it is warm, then it becomes red-hot and glows with marvelous beauty, and you have the cold bar of iron glowing with fire.

You and I are cold—oh, how cold we are—and the Lord Jesus takes us and He plunges us into the fire of the Holy Spirit. We begin to grow warm, and soon we glow, glow with love to God, glow with love to Christ, glow with love to the truth, glow with love for perishing souls. Men and women, the great need of the day is men and women on fire. Brethren, that is what we need in the pulpit, ministers on fire. What cold men most of us preachers are! Orthodox enough, it may be, and we present the most solemn truth with great force of reason and great beauty of rhetoric and most convincing eloquence; and our audiences sit there and admire our strong preaching, but they do not repent of their sins. Why not? Because we are not on fire. We convince the intellect, but we do not melt the heart. But put a minister who is on fire in the pulpit, and the audience will melt. Wesley was such a man, Whitefield was such a man; Charles G. Finney was such a man.

We need that kind of person in the choir as well. What beautiful choirs we have nowadays. Why, they sing almost like angels, and people sit there admiring them, but nobody is converted by their singing. But when we get a man on fire to sing, or a woman on fire to sing, or a choir on fire to sing, something is brought to pass. That is what we need in our Sunday school classes. We set a young man or a young woman to teach a Sunday school class. Many know the lesson capitally and study all the latest "helps," and make the lesson tremendously interesting, but the boys and girls and men and women in their classes are not converted, because the teachers are not on fire. Oh, men and women of London, the need in London more than anything else tonight is a baptism with fire on the minister, a baptism with fire on the elders, a baptism with fire on the deacons, a baptism with fire on the choir, a baptism with fire on the Sunday school teachers, and a baptism with fire upon the men and women in the congregation. We sang a hymn just now, praying that the fire of God might fall in Mildmay Conference Hall tonight. If it does, men and women, if it does, London will be shaken.

6. Fire Imparts Energy

The next thing that fire does is impart energy. The men of science tell us that every form of energy can be transmuted into fire, and that given fire you can generate any form of force or energy. When a baptism with fire comes, then comes power. That was the principal manifestation at Pentecost. The fire of God fell, and with the energy of that fire, men went out from that upper room, and 3,000 people were converted.

A man takes me to his factory. He says, "This machinery is the best in the world." He takes me down into the engine room and says, "Look at that great engine, it is so many horsepower, and there is power in that engine to move every wheel in this great factory." Then I go back to the factory and I look around. There is nothing doing at all.

"It is very strange," I say; "did you not tell me that this was the best machinery in the world for this purpose, and that that engine downstairs could move every wheel in the factory? Well, I notice the connections are all made, and everything is in gear, and the lever is carried the right way, but there is not a wheel moving in all the factory. What is the matter?"

"Don't you know?" he says. "Come downstairs, and I will show you," and he takes me down again to the engine room to the engine, and he throws open the door and says, "Look in there." And lo! There is no fire in the firebox.

I go off to the railway. There is a great engine standing on the rails, and I am told it is the finest engine that was ever turned out from the locomotive works. It can drag a heavily freighted train up a hundred-foot grade. The engine has been coupled on to about half-a-dozen unloaded cars. I look at the engine and say, "What did you tell me? Can it draw a heavily loaded train up a hundred-foot grade? Then will you please explain something to me? That engine has only six empty cars behind it, the coupling is made, the throttle is open, and yet it is not moving, and cannot pull a car, and yet you say it can pull a hundred. What is the matter?" I am taken on to the engine, and the door of the furnace is thrown open, and when I look in I see there is no fire in the firebox. That is what is the matter.

Friends, I go into churches today, and oh, what beautiful organization I see, what magnificent architecture, what eloquent preaching I hear, what marvelous singing! And yet not a wheel in the whole institution moving for God. What is the matter? There is no fire in the firebox. What we need today is the fire of God in the firebox, and thank God the promise is, "He shall baptize you with the Holy Ghost, and fire."

7. Fire Spreads

One thing more about this fire—fire spreads. Nothing spreads like fire. I remember hearing some years ago, before I went to live in Chicago, about an old Irish woman, who had a little shanty in the city, with a little shed back of it, in which she kept a cow. And one night she was milking her cow, and the cow suddenly kicked and knocked over her lantern. The lantern fell on a wisp of straw, which caught fire, and set the shed afire. The shed set the shanty afire, and the shanty next to it caught fire, and the shanty next to that and the one next to that, and soon the fire leaped over the south branch of the Chicago River to the east side. On and on it swept, and in forty-eight hours it had cleared an area one mile wide and three miles long, and there were but two buildings left in all that section of Chicago. Fire spreads. If a fire is kindled here tonight, it will sweep all over London, and all over Great Britain, and Ireland.

That night I spoke of at the beginning of my sermon, we had a stranger from London in Chicago, who came to hear me preach. He came downstairs in response to my invitation, and he told us, "I am just in Chicago today from London, and I want this baptism of fire"; and he got it. When he left the church, he went to his room and sat down and wrote a letter to the Bible class of which he was a member in London. The teacher read it to the class, and the fire of God came into that class, and in about two weeks after he had sent the letter, he got word from London that the fire that fell in Chicago had been kindled in that church in London.

Nothing spreads like fire. Do we not need the baptism with this fire tonight?

The Fire of Judgment That Tests Believers' Works

You will find the second fire in 1 Corinthians 3:13, 15: "Every man's work shall be made manifest: for the day shall declare it, because it shall be revealed by fire; and the fire shall try every man's work of what sort it is. . . . If any man's work shall be burned, he shall suffer loss: but he himself shall be saved; yet so as by fire." This second fire is the fire of judgment, testing our works at the judgment seat of Christ.

Now you notice the judgment here is not the judgment regarding our salvation. These are saved people whose works are burnt up. All the work we do for Christ is to be put to the test, is to be put to the severest kind of test, the fire test; and, friends, there is a great deal the church of Christ is doing professedly for Christ, and a great deal individual Christians are doing, that will never stand the fire test. A great deal of work that is good, but that is done not to God's glory but for personal ambition—the good sermon, perfectly orthodox, severely logical, beautifully rhetorical, the sermon that even good people applaud, but that is preached not that God may be glorified in the salvation of sinners but that the preacher may be applauded—will that stand the fire test? Never! It will go up in smoke. The beautiful solos sung, the philanthropic work done, the personal soul-saving work done, not for God's glory but for the exaltation of self—will these stand the fire test? Never! They will all go up in smoke.

On the night of which I have been speaking in my church, the two leading singers went down into that second meeting, and the leading soprano said—a beautiful singer, one of the most beautiful singers I have ever heard, "I never thought of it before. I don't believe I have sung a solo in my life for God. I sang it for self." Thank God the fire of God came upon my leading soprano and my leading contralto, and I lost them both, for they became missionaries. I would like to lose the whole choir, if I could lose them in the same way!

Furthermore, let me say, good work, work done for a good purpose, but done in our own strength and not done in the power of the Holy Ghost, will not stand the fire test. The sermon preached to glorify God, but preached with the enticing words of man's wisdom and not in demonstration of the spirit and power of God, will never stand the fire test. So, men and women, our work is to be tried regarding its character, regarding its motive, regarding its power in which it is done. Will your work stand the fire?

The Fire of Eternal Doom

We come now to the third fire. We read of it in 2 Thessalonians 1:7–9: "The Lord Jesus shall be revealed from heaven with his mighty angels, in flaming fire taking vengeance on them that know not God, and that obey not the gospel of our Lord Jesus Christ: Who shall be punished with everlasting destruction from the presence of the Lord, and from the glory of his power." The third fire is the fire of eternal doom. Every one of us must meet God in fire somewhere. Some of us, I hope, tonight will meet Him in the fire of baptism with the Holy Ghost and fire; some of us, I know, will meet Him in that great Judgment Day, when the fire will try our work, of what sort it is; and oh, friends, some of us, I fear—God grant it may be very few—may meet Him in the fire of eternal doom.

Someone says, "Do you think it is literal fire?" I will not stop to discuss that. Take it as a figure if you will, but remember that figures always stand for facts. Some people, if they find anything in the Bible that they do not like, say, "It is figurative," and they think that has swept it all away. Remember, who uses the figures; they are God's figures; and God's figures stand for facts, and God is not a liar, so God's figures never overstate the facts they represent. And how terrible must be the mental and spiritual agony described by that figure, if figure it be! Were you ever severely burnt? Did you ever see anyone severely burnt? I have. And how awful must be the spiritual or physical agony, whichever it is, that is represented by such a terrible figure as this.

The superficial thinker says, "Oh, I cannot believe that; I cannot believe that a merciful God is going to let men go on suffering day after day, week after week, month after month, and year after year, with no hope." Open your eyes. Look at what is going on right around you in London. Is not God permitting men and women who sin, especially in certain specific forms of sin, to suffer the most awful agonies day after day, month after month, year after year, without one hope of relief unless they repent; and when the time of possible repentance is passed—and it must pass sometime—when the time of possible repentance is passed, what have you got but hell? You don't get rid of hell by getting rid of the Bible, or by getting rid of God; hell is here; hell is a fact in London tonight. The only change the Bible and God make is that they open a door of hope, and when you banish God and the Bible the only change you make is that you shut the only door of hope.

The infidels are guilty of the amazing folly of trying to close hell by shutting the only door of hope. Hell is here. It is a present-day fact, and unless there is repentance and acceptance of Christ, it will be an eternal and endless fact. You say, "For whom?" Listen: "Taking vengeance on them that know not God, and that obey not the gospel" (2 Thessalonians 1:8).

First, "on them that know not God." That is plain English for agnostics. Do you know what "agnostic" means? A great many people are proud of saying, "I am an agnostic." Well, agnostic means "know not" or "know nothing"; it is used of those who "know not God." So our text says God will render vengeance to agnostics. Someone says, "That is not just." I cannot help that: it is a fact. But it is just. You ought to know God; you have no excuse for not knowing God. The most solemn duty that lies upon every man is to find out about God, and there is a way to know God. The trouble is you don't want to know God. Any agnostic that wants to know God will soon get acquainted with Him. I was once an agnostic, but I was an honest one, and I did not take long to find God.

Only the other night a man said to me, "I am an agnostic." I pointed him to a way out of agnosticism, a reasonable way, and asked, "Is not that reasonable?" and he said, "Yes." Then I said, "Will you try it?" and he said, "No, I won't." His agnosticism is not his misfortune; it is his sin. The first and most solemn obligation resting on the creature is to know and worship and serve the Creator. You ought to know God, and if you refuse to know Him, the Lord Jesus will be revealed at last rendering vengeance to you and other agnostics.

But not only to agnostics but to them "that obey not the gospel." Many a man is not an agnostic, but he does not obey the

Gospel. There are many of you people who would support what I say about agnosticism, but you do not obey the Gospel. You do not believe with real faith, which means absolute surrender to and confidence in the Lord Jesus Christ. You do not obey Jesus Christ as your Lord and Master. You do not openly confess Him as the Gospel commands. He will render vengeance to you; you shall be "punished with everlasting destruction from the presence of the Lord, and from the glory of his power."

Men and women, every one of us must meet God in fire. Oh, tonight do you not want to meet Him in the glorious fire of the Holy Ghost, refining you from sin, cleansing the dross and filth, illuminating you with God's glorious truth, warming the cold heart until it glows with holy love, energizing you with the power of God, and spreading wherever it goes? Or do you wish to meet God in fire at that Judgment Day, that will try your work as to character, motive, the power that wrought it, and send all your works up in smoke, and leave you there stripped, saved "so as by fire?" Or will you meet God in that awful fire of eternal doom, when the day comes that the same Christ whom you have rejected and trampled underfoot comes back again in the glory of the Father, with His mighty angels, "taking vengeance to them that know not God, and that obey not the gospel"?

7

What the Resurrection of Jesus from the Dead Proves

AT THE PODIUM

This sermon is a perfect example of Torrey's balanced use of apologetics in evangelism. It comes after a series of sermons arguing for the historical credibility of the resurrection of Christ, and turns the corner to explore the implications of the resurrection. First he presents evidence for its truth and then warms to his subject when he argues the implications.

Source: R. A. Torrey. "What the Resurrection of Jesus from the Dead Proves." *The Bible and Its Christ: Being Noonday Talks with Business Men on Faith and Unbelief.* New York: Revell, 1904, 101–11.

In our last three addresses we have seen conclusive evidence that Jesus Christ rose from the dead. We have followed a number of independent lines of argument. Several of these taken alone satisfactorily prove the fact of the resurrection, but taken together they constitute an argument that makes doubt of the resurrection of

Christ impossible to a candid mind. But suppose He did rise from the dead, what of it? What does His resurrection prove? It proves everything that most needs to be proved. It proves everything that is essential in Christianity.

The Resurrection Proves There Is One True God

First of all, *the resurrection of Christ from the dead proves that there is a God, and that the God of the Bible is the true God.* Every effect must have an adequate cause, and the only adequate cause that will account for the resurrection of Jesus Christ is God, the God of the Bible.

When Jesus was here upon earth, He proclaimed the God of the Bible, "the God of Abraham, Isaac, and Jacob," the God of the Old Testament as well as the New. He claimed that after men had put Him to death, the God of Abraham, Isaac, and Jacob, the God of the Bible, would raise Him from the dead the third day. This was a stupendous claim to make, apparently an absurd claim. For centuries men had come and gone; they had lived and died, and as far as human observation went, that was the end of them; but Jesus claimed that after all these centuries of men living, dying, and passing into oblivion, that God, the God of the Bible, would raise Him from the dead. Jesus died; He was crucified, dead, and buried; the appointed hour at which He had claimed God would raise Him from the dead came. God did raise Him from the dead, and thereby Jesus' astounding claim was substantiated, and it was decisively proven that there is a God, and that the God of the Bible is the true God.

For centuries men have been seeking for proofs of the existence and character of God. There is the teleological argument, the argument from the marks of creative intelligence and design in the material universe; a good argument in its place. There is the argument from the intelligent guiding hand of God in human history; the ontological argument, and other arguments, all more or less convincing; but the resurrection of Jesus Christ from the dead provides us with a solid, scientific foundation for our faith in God.

In the light of the resurrection, our faith in God is built upon observed facts. In the light of the resurrection of Jesus, atheism and agnosticism have no longer any standing ground. Well might Peter say, "[We] through Him are believers in God, [who] raised Him from the dead, and gave Him glory" (1 Peter. 1:21 RV).

My belief in the God of the Bible is not a felicitous fancy. It is a fixed faith resting upon an incontrovertibly firm fact.

The Resurrection Proves Jesus Spoke the Very Words of God

Second, *the resurrection of Jesus Christ from the dead proves that Jesus is a teacher sent from God, who received His message from God, that He was absolutely inerrant, that He spoke the very words of God.* This was Jesus' claim for Himself. In John 7:16 He says, "My teaching is not Mine, but His that sent Me" (RV). In John 12:49 He says, "I have not spoken of myself; but the Father which sent me, he gave me a commandment, what I should say, and what I should speak." In John 14:10–11 He says, "Believest thou not that I am in the Father, and the Father in me? the words that I speak unto you I speak not of myself: but the Father that dwelleth in me, he doeth the works. Believe me that I am in the Father, and the Father in me: or else believe me for the very works' sake." In John 14:24 He says, "The word which ye hear is not mine, but the Father's which sent me." His claim was that His words were the very words of God.

This, too, was a stupendous claim to make. Others have made similar claims, but the difference between their claims and those of Jesus is that Jesus substantiated His claims, and no one else has ever substantiated his. God Himself unmistakably set His seal upon this astounding claim of Jesus Christ by raising Him from the dead. In the light of the resurrection of Jesus Christ from the dead, that school of criticism that assumes to question the absolute inerrancy of Jesus Christ as a teacher, and to set its authority up above that of Jesus, has absolutely no standing ground. Yea, further, that school of criticism, by putting forward its unsubstantiated claims in opposition to the demonstrated claims of Jesus Christ, makes itself a laughingstock in the eyes of thoughtful men.

The Resurrection Proves Jesus Is the Son of God

Third, *the resurrection of Jesus Christ from the dead proves that He is the Son of God*. The apostle Paul says, in Romans 1:4, that He is "declared to be the Son of God with power . . . by the resurrection from the dead." Anyone who will stop to think will see that this is beyond a peradventure true. When Jesus was here upon earth, He claimed to be divine in a sense in which no other man was divine. He taught that while even the greatest of God's prophets were only servants, He was a Son, an only Son (Mark 12:6; note context). He claimed that He and the Father were one (John 10:30), and that all men should honor Him, even as they honored the Father (John 5:23); that He was so completely and fully indwelt of God, such a perfect and absolute incarnation of God, that he that had seen Him had seen the Father (John 14:9). This was a most amazing claim to make, a claim that, if not true, was rankest blasphemy. He told men that they would put Him to death, for making this claim, but that after they had put Him to death, God Himself would set His seal to the claim by raising Him from the dead.

They did put Him to death for making this claim; the disbelievers in the deity of Jesus Christ of that day caused Him to be nailed to the cross of Calvary for claiming to be divine (Matthew 26:63–66); but when the appointed hour had come, the breath of God swept through the sleeping clay, and God Himself, as Jesus claimed He would, set His seal to Christ's assertion of His own deity by raising Him from the dead. God thus proclaimed to all ages, with clearer voice than if He should speak from the open heavens today, "This is My only begotten Son, the One in whom I dwell in all My fullness, so that he that hath seen Him hath seen the Father." In the light of the resurrection of Jesus Christ from the dead, Unitarianism has absolutely no logical standing ground.

The Resurrection Proves There Is a Judgment Day Coming

Fourth, *the resurrection of Jesus Christ from the dead proves that there is a Judgment Day coming*. On Mars Hill Paul declared "he hath appointed a day, in the which he will judge the world in righteousness by that man whom he hath ordained; whereof he hath given assurance unto all men, in that he hath raised him from the dead" (Acts 17:31), thus making the resurrection of Christ the God-given assurance of the coming judgment.

But how does the resurrection of Christ give assurance of coming judgment? When Jesus was upon earth, He declared that the Father had committed all judgment unto Him. He declared further that the hour was coming in which all that were in their graves should hear His voice and come forth; they that had done good unto the resurrection of life, and they that had done evil unto the resurrection of judgment (John 5:22, 28–29). Men ridiculed His claim, hated Him for making the claim, put Him to death for making the claim and the other claim involved in it, that of deity. But God set His seal to the claim by raising Him from the dead.

The resurrection of Jesus Christ from the dead, which is an absolutely certain fact of history in the past, points with unerring finger to an absolutely certain coming judgment in the future. Belief in a coming Judgment Day is no guess of theologians. It is a positive faith founded upon a proven fact. In the light of the resurrection of Jesus Christ from the dead, the man who continues in sin, flattering himself with the hope that there will be no future day of reckoning and of judgment, is guilty of madness. Jesus will sit in judgment, and every one of us must give account to Him of the deeds done in the body.

The Resurrection Proves Every Believer Is Justified from All Things

Fifth, *the resurrection of Jesus Christ from the dead proves that every believer in Christ is justified from all things.* We read in Romans 4:25 (RV) that Jesus "was delivered up for our trespasses, and was raised for our justification." More literally, "He was delivered up because of our trespasses [that is, because we had trespassed], and was raised because of our justification [that is, because we were justified]." The resurrection of Jesus Christ proves decisively that the believer in Him is justified. But how? When Jesus was on earth He said that He would offer up His life "a ransom for many" (Matthew 20:28). The hour came, He offered up His life on the cross of Calvary as a ransom for us. Now the atonement has been made, but there still remains a question, "Will God accept the atonement that has thus been offered?"

For three nights and three days, this question remains unanswered. Jesus lies in the grave, cold and dead. The long predicted hour comes, the breath of God sweeps through that sleeping clay, and Christ rises triumphant from the dead and is exalted to the right hand of the Father, and God proclaims to the whole universe, "I have accepted the atonement which Jesus made." When Jesus died, He died as my representative, and I died in Him; when He arose, He rose as my representative, and I arose in Him; when He ascended up on high and took His place at the right hand of the Father in the glory, He ascended as my representative and I ascended in Him—and today I am seated in Christ with God in the heavenlies.

I look at the cross of Christ, and I know that atonement has been made for my sins; I look at the open sepulcher and the risen and ascended Lord, and I know that the atonement has been accepted. There no longer remains a single sin on me, no matter how many or how great my sins may have been. My sins may have been as high as the mountains, but in the light of the resurrection, the atonement that covers them is as high as heaven. My sins may have been as deep as the ocean, but in the light of the resurrection, the atonement that swallows them up is as deep as eternity. "Be it known unto you therefore, men and brethren, that through this man is preached unto you the forgiveness of sins: And by him all that believe are justified from all things" (Acts 13:38–39).

The Resurrection Proves Those United to Christ Shall Live Again

In the sixth place, *the resurrection of Jesus Christ from the dead proves that all who are united to Christ by a living faith shall live again.* Paul says, "If we believe that Jesus died and rose again, even so them also which sleep in Jesus will God bring with him" (1 Thessalonians 4:14). The believer is so united to Christ by a living faith that if Christ rose, we must. If the grave could not hold Him, it cannot hold us.

For centuries men have been seeking proofs of immortality. We have had the dreams of poets and the speculations of philosophers to cheer us with the hope that we shall live again, but the best of philosophical arguments only point to the probability of a future life. In a matter like this, the human heart craves and demands something more than a probability. In the resurrection of Jesus Christ, we get something more than probability—we get absolute certainty; we get scientific demonstration of life beyond the grave. The resurrection of Jesus Christ removes the hope of immortality from the domain of the speculative and the probable into the domain of the scientifically demonstrated and certain. We know there is a life beyond the grave.

A popular preacher has recently said, "Not a few are not at all sure that there is any life beyond the grave. They wish it could be proven. So do I. But we can do no more than infer it from the moral constitution of the universe." Thank God, this popular preacher is wrong. Before the resurrection of Jesus Christ, perhaps, we could "do no more than infer it from the moral constitution of the universe," but in the light of the resurrection, it is no longer left to uncertain inferences from the moral constitution of the universe; it is proven. No further proof is needed. It is scientifically demonstrated, and to anyone who will candidly ponder the facts regarding the resurrection of Christ, unbelief or agnosticism in regard to the future life becomes an impossibility. In the light of the first Easter morning, I go out into the cemeteries where lies the sleeping dust of father and mother, brother, child, and all my tears are brushed away, for I hear the Father saying, Thy father shall live again; thy mother shall live again; thy brother shall live again; thy child shall live again.

The Resurrection Proves a Believer Can Have Hourly Victory over Sin

Seventh, *the resurrection of Jesus Christ from the dead proves that it is the believer's privilege to have daily, hourly, constant victory over sin.* We are united not only to the Lord who died, and thus made atonement for our sin, and thus delivered us from the guilt of sin; we are united to the Lord who rose again, who "ever liveth to make intercession for [us]," and who has power to save to the uttermost, power to keep us from falling day by day, "and to present [us] faultless before the presence of his glory with exceeding joy" (Hebrews 7:25; Jude 24).

I may be weak, utterly weak, unable to resist temptation for a single hour, but He is strong, infinitely strong, and He lives to give me help and deliverance every day and every hour. The question of victory over sin is not a question of my weakness but of His strength, His resurrection power, always at my disposal. He has all power in heaven and on earth, and what my risen Lord has belongs to me also. In the light of the resurrection of Jesus Christ from the dead, failure in daily living is unnecessary and inexcusable. In His resurrection life and power, it is our privilege and our duty to lead victorious lives.

Four men were once climbing the slippery side of the Matterhorn, a guide and a tourist, a second guide and a second tourist, all roped together. The lower tourist lost his footing and went over the side. The sudden pull on the rope carried the lower guide with him, and he carried the other tourist with him. Three men were now dangling over the dizzy cliff. But the guide who was in the lead, feeling the first pull upon the rope, drove his pike into the ice, braced his feet, and held fast; three men dangling over the awful abyss, but three men safe, because they were tied to the man that held fast. The first tourist regained his place, the guide regained his, and the lower tourist regained his, and on and up they went in safety.

As the human race ascended the icy cliffs of life, the first Adam lost his footing and swept over the abyss. He pulled the next man after him, and the next, and the next, and the next, until the whole race hung over the abyss. But the second Adam, the Man in the glory, stood fast, and all who are united to Him by a living faith, though dangling over the awful precipice, are safe, because they are tied to the Man in the glory.

8

God's Blockade of the Road to Hell

AT THE PODIUM

Asking "What must I do to be saved?" is one way of approaching the message of salvation, though it is a question that needs to be reoriented lest it be taken to mean "What work can I do to earn salvation?" This classic Torrey sermon flips the question to "What must I do to be damned?" It takes its start from an evangelical Arminian way of putting things: that God wants you to be saved and has put many obstacles between you and damnation.

Source: From R. A. Torrey. "God's Blockade of the Road to Hell." *Real Salvation and Whole-Hearted Service.* New York: Revell, 1905, 60–70.

If any man or woman in this audience is lost, it won't be God's fault. God does not wish you to be lost. God longs to have you saved. "The Lord is not willing that any should perish, but that all should come to repentance," the apostle Peter wrote (2 Peter 3:9). If God had His way, every man and woman in this audience would not only be saved sometime but saved tonight. God is doing everything in His power to bring you men and women to repentance.

Of course, He cannot save you if you will not repent. You can have salvation if you want to be saved from sin, but sin and salvation can never go together. There are people who talk about a scheme of salvation whereby man can continue in sin and yet be saved. It is impossible. Sin is damnation, and if a man will go on everlastingly in sin, he will be everlastingly lost. But God is doing everything in His power to turn you out of the path of sin and destruction into the path of righteousness and everlasting life. God has filled the path of sin—the path that leads to hell—with obstacles. He has made it hard and bitter. A great many people are saying today, "The Christian life is so hard." It is not. Christ's "yoke is easy, and [his] burden is light" (Matthew 11:30). God tells us in His Word, "The way of transgressors is hard" (Proverbs 13:15). God has filled it full of obstacles, and you cannot go on in it without surmounting one obstacle after another. I am to talk to you tonight about some of the obstacles that God has put in the path of sin and ruin.

Obstacle One: The Bible

The first one is *the Bible*. You cannot get very far in the path of sin without finding the Bible in your way. The Bible is one of the greatest hindrances to sin in the world. With its warnings, with its invitations, with its descriptions of the character and consequences of sin, with its representations of its beauty, and its reward, with its pictures of God and God's love, the Bible always stands as a great hindrance to sin. It makes men uneasy in sin. That is the reason many men hate the Bible; they are determined to sin, and the Bible makes them uneasy in sin, so they hate the Book.

Men will give you a great many reasons why they object to the Bible, but in ninety-nine cases out of one hundred, if you should trace men's objections to the Bible home, you would find the reason they hate the Bible is because it makes them uneasy in their sin. Men sometimes say to me, "I object to the Bible because of its filthy stories," but when I look into their lives, I find that their lives are filthy, and that their real objection is not to filthy stories, of which there are none. Stories of sin there are; stories that paint sin in its true colors; stories that make sin hideous—and their objection is not to filthy stories but because the Bible makes them uneasy in their filthy lives. This is why you hate it. The Bible makes it hard for you to go on in sin.

How often a man has been turned back from the path of sin by a single verse in the Bible. Hundreds of men have been turned out of the path of sin by Romans 6:23, "The wages of sin is death; but the gift of God is eternal life through Jesus Christ our Lord." Thousands of men have been turned out of the path of sin by Amos 4:12, "Prepare to meet thy God." Tens of thousands of men have been turned out of the path of sin by John 3:16, "For God so loved the world, that he gave his only begotten Son, that whosoever believeth in him should not perish, but have everlasting life." And John 6:37, "Him that cometh to me I will in no wise cast out."

Several years ago a man came into our church in Chicago, who had not been in a house of worship for fifteen or sixteen years. He was a rampant infidel. I don't know why he came in that night. I suppose because he saw the crowd coming and was curious to know what was going on. He sat down, and I began to preach. In my sermon, I quoted John 6:37, "Him that cometh to me I will in no wise cast out." It went like an arrow into that man's heart. When the meeting was over he got up and went out, and tried to forget that verse but could not. He went to bed but could not sleep. "Him that cometh to me I will in no wise cast out" kept ringing in his mind. The next day it haunted him at work, and the next and the next, and for days and weeks that verse haunted him, but he was bound not to come to Christ.

He came back to the street where our church stands, walked up and down the sidewalk, stamped his foot, and cursed the text, but he could not get rid of it. Six weeks passed and he came into our prayer meeting, and stood up and said, "Men and women, I was here six weeks ago and heard your minister preach. I heard the text,

John 6:37, and I have tried to forget it, but it has haunted me night and day. I have walked up and down the sidewalk in front of your church. I have stamped on the sidewalk and cursed the text, but I can't get rid of it. Pray for me." And we did, and he was saved. One text from God's Word turned him out of the path of sin and ruin.

Obstacle Two: A Mother's Influence and Teaching

The second obstacle that God has put in the path of sin is *a mother's holy influence and a mother's teaching.*

How many hundreds of men and women there are here tonight who are not yet Christians, who have tried to be infidels, tried to plunge down into sin, but your mother's holy influence and your mother's Christian teaching won't let you go the way you wish to.

Sometimes it is years afterward that a mother's teaching does its work. We had in America a young fellow who went west to Colorado in the mining times. He worked in the mines during the day and gambled at night, as so many miners do, but he spent more money gambling than he made in the mines. One night he was at the gaming table. He lost his last cent. Then he used some of his employer's money and lost that. He felt he was ruined. He arose from the gaming table, went up into the mountains, drew his revolver and held it to his temple, and was about to pull the trigger, when a word that his mother had spoken to him years before came to his mind, "My son, if you are ever in trouble, think of God." And there, standing in the moonlight, with a revolver pressed against his temple, and his finger upon the trigger of the revolver, and the revolver cocked, he remembered what his mother had said, and dropped on his knees, and cried to God and was saved. Turned out of the path of perdition by a mother's teaching.

Obstacle Three: A Mother's Prayers

Another obstacle that God has put in the path of sin and ruin is *a mother's prayers.* Oh, men, in the desperate hardness of our hearts, we often trample our mother's teaching underfoot, but we find it very hard to get over her prayers. How often at the last moment a man is saved by his mother's prayers.

I have in my church in Chicago a man who stood outside the tabernacle in the old days with a pitcher of beer, and as the people came out of the meeting, he offered them drink out of that pitcher of beer. He was hard and desperate and wicked. He had a praying mother in Scotland. One night when he went home from the meeting where he had caused trouble, in the middle of the night, in answer to the prayers of a godly mother in Scotland, he was awakened and saved without getting out of bed. He came back to Scotland to see his mother. He had a brother who was a sailor in the China seas, and the mother and the saved son knelt down and prayed for the wandering boy, and that very night while they prayed, the Spirit of God came down upon that sailor and he was saved and afterward became Dr. Morrison, a missionary to India—saved by a mother's prayers.

I stand here tonight a saved man, because when I was rushing headlong in the path of sin and ruin, my mother's prayers arose and I could not get over them. I used to think that nobody had anything to do with my salvation, no living being, for I was awakened in the middle of the night. I had gone to bed with no more thought of becoming a Christian than I had of jumping over the moon. In the middle of the night I jumped out of bed and started to end my miserable life, but something came upon me, and I dropped on my knees, and in five minutes from the time I got out of bed to take my life I had surrendered to God. I thought no man or woman had anything to with it, but I found out a woman had—my mother 427 miles away praying, and while I had gotten over sermons and arguments and churches, and everything else, I could not get over my mother's prayers. Do you know why some of you men are not in hell tonight? Your mother's prayers have kept you out of hell.

Obstacle Four: A Certain Sermon

Another obstacle is the sermons we hear. How many thousands are turned back from sin to God by sermons that they hear or read. Sometimes the sermon does its work years afterward.

I remember once, in my first pastorate, I prepared a sermon on the parable of the ten virgins. There was one member of my congregation who was very much on my heart—I prayed that the woman might be saved by that sermon. I went and preached the sermon. I fully expected to see her saved by that sermon, but when I gave the invitation she never made sign. I went home and did not know what to make of it. I said, "I prayed for her conversion by that sermon and fully expected her conversion, and she is not converted.'" Years afterward, when I had gone to another pastorate, I heard that this woman was converted. I revisited the place and called upon her, and said, "I am very glad to hear you have been converted." She said, "Would you like to know how I was converted?" I said I would. "Do you remember preaching a sermon years ago on the ten virgins? When you preached that sermon, I could not get it out of my mind. I felt I must take Christ that night, but I would not, and that sermon followed me, and I was converted years after by that sermon." I was sure she was going to be converted by the sermon. But I did not see it for years.

Obstacle Five: A Teacher's Influence

Another obstacle is a Sunday school teacher's influence and teaching. How many it brings to Christ! How many in this audience tonight were brought to Christ by the teaching of a faithful Christian man or woman in the Sunday school? I want to say to you Sunday school teachers that a faithful Sunday school teacher is one of God's best instruments on earth for the salvation of the perishing.

In Mr. Moody's first Sunday school in Chicago he had a class of very unruly girls—nobody could manage them—but finally he found a young man who did manage them. One day this young man came into Mr. Moody's shop (it was before Mr. Moody left business) and said, "Mr. Moody " (and he burst into tears). Mr. Moody said, "What is the matter?"

"The doctor says I have consumption, and that I must go to California at once or die," and he sobbed as if his heart would break. Mr. Moody tried to comfort him and said, "Suppose that is so, you have no occasion to feel so bad. You are a Christian."

"It is not that, Mr. Moody; I am perfectly willing to die, I am not afraid to die, but here I have had this Sunday school class all these years and not one of them saved, and I am going off to leave them, every one unsaved," and he sobbed like a child.

Mr. Moody said, "Wait, I will get a carriage and we will drive around and visit them, and one by one you can lead them to Christ." He took the pale teacher in the carriage and they drove around to the homes of the girls, and he talked to them about Christ until he was so tired that he had to be taken home. The next day they went out again, and they went out every day until every one of these women but one was saved.

Then they met for a prayer meeting before he went away. One after another led in prayer, and at last the one unsaved girl in the whole company led in prayer too and accepted Christ. He left by the early train the next morning, and Mr. Moody went down to the train to see him off. As they were waiting, one by one the girls dropped in, without any prearrangement, until every one of the young women was on the platform. He spoke a few words of farewell to them, and as the train pulled out of the station, he stood upon the back platform of the car with his finger pointing heavenward, telling his Sunday school class to meet him in heaven.

A Sixth Obstacle: A Kind Word or Act

One obstacle God often throws in the path of sin is a *kind word or act*. A lady friend of mine was standing in a window looking out on Bleecker Street in New York. A drunkard came down the street. He had been a man in high circumstances; he had been the mayor of a Southern city but had gone down through drink, and was now a penniless drunkard on the streets of New York. He had made up his mind to commit suicide. He started for the river, but as he was going down Bleecker Street he thought, "I will go into a public-house and have one more drink. I have spent a lot of money in that public-house, and I can certainly stand the man off for one drink." He went in and asked for a drink, and told the man he had no money to pay for it, and the man came around from behind the bar and kicked him into the gutter.

My friend, looking out of the window, saw the poor wretch picking himself up out of the gutter, and she crossed over and wiped the mud off with her handkerchief, and said, "Come over in there. It is bright and warm and you will be welcome at our meeting." The poor wretch went over and sat down behind the stove. The meeting began, and one after another gave their testimony. When the meeting was over that lady came and spoke to him about his soul, and his heart was touched and he was saved. He got one position and then a better one, and finally was made manager of one of the largest publishing houses in the city of New York.

One day he came to my friend and said, "I have some friends down at a hotel; I want you to meet them." She went to the hotel, and he introduced her to a fine-looking, middle-aged woman and a fine-looking young lady, and said, "This is my wife and daughter"—beautiful, refined, cultured ladies whom he had left and gone down to the very verge of hell; but a kind act and a word of invitation to Christ had turned him out of the path to perdition. He had been within one step of hell but entered the path that leads to glory. Oh, let us go as the missionaries of God's grace and block the path of sinful men and women with kindly deeds, and thus turn them to righteousness and to God.

A Seventh Obstacle: The Holy Spirit

Another obstacle that God puts in the path of sin and ruin is the Holy Spirit and His work. How strange it is. You and I have experienced it. When we were right in the midst of a carousal, a strange feeling came into our heart, an unrest, a dissatisfaction with the life we were living, a longing for something better, memories of home, church, mother, Bible, and God.

A man one night was playing cards at the table. He was a man wholly given up to the world, belonged to one of your noble families, not a nobleman himself but connected with members of the nobility—a wild, reckless, English spendthrift, and there he sat playing cards, and suddenly the voice of God's Spirit spoke in his heart. He thought he was about to die. He sprang up from the table, threw down his cards, rushed to his room. There was someone in the room. He thought at first, "It won't do to pray while the maid is in the room." But he was so much in earnest that he did not mind anybody. He dropped down by his bed and called upon God for Christ's sake to forgive his sins. That man was Brownlow North, who did such a great work for God in Ireland and Scotland in 1859 and '60.

Oh, friends, listen. Last night as you were in some den of infamy, there came into your heart a wretchedness, a sense of self-disgust, a longing for something better, a calling to a purer life—what was it? God's Spirit. As you sit in this place here tonight (all over this building), there is a stirring in your heart, and you are saying to yourself, "I wonder I had better not become a Christian tonight?" Almost a determination to stand up as soon as the invitation is given out. What is it? God sending His Spirit to blockade the road to hell. Listen, men, listen to God's Spirit tonight. Yield; accept Christ.

A Final Obstacle: The Cross of Christ

God has put one other obstacle in the path to hell: the cross of Christ. No man can get very far down the path of sin and ruin until he sees looming before him the cross. On that cross there hangs a Man—the Son of Man, the Son of God. There you see Him hanging with nails in His hands and feet, and a voice says, "It was for you. I bore this for you. I died for you."

In the pathway of every man and woman here tonight stands the cross with Christ upon it, and if you go out of Bingley Hall to continue in sin, you will have to go over the cross and over the crucified form of the Son of God.

I heard of a godly old man who had a worthless son. That son was more anxious to make money than he was for honor or anything else, and he determined to go into that infamous business in which there is lots of money, but which no self-respecting man will undertake, the liquor business. Any man who is willing to coin money out of rum selling will coin money out of the tears of brokenhearted wives, out of the groans and sighs of the drunkards' sons and daughters, out of the heart's blood of their fellow men, for this infernal rum traffic is sending thousands of men every year to premature graves. This infernal rum traffic is causing more sorrow, more ruined homes, more wretchedness than perhaps anything else on earth, and every publican, every barman, every barmaid, and every professed Christian that holds stocks in breweries or distilleries, every one of you is a party to the crime. You have plenty to say about the rum-seller and the bartender. I would like to know how he is any worse than you professed Christians who own brewery stocks. He gets the abuse and you get the money, and you will get the eternal damnation unless you get out of the infernal business.

Well, this man so far lost his self-respect that he was going to open a public-house, and his father was ashamed. He pled with him. He said, "My boy, you bear an honored name that has never been disgraced before. Don't disgrace it by putting it up over a public-house." But the son was so bent on moneymaking that he would not listen to his father's voice.

The day came to open the public-house. The father was about the first on hand. He stood outside the door of that public-house, and every man that approached the door he stepped up to him and told him of the miseries that came from strong drink, warned him of the consequences of entering such a place as that, and, one after another, they turned away. The son looked out of the window to see why he was getting no customers. He saw his father outside, turning his customers away. He came outside and said, "Father, go home. You are ruining my business." He said, "I cannot help it, my boy. I won't have my name dishonored by this business, and if you are bent on going on with it, I will stand here and warn every man that comes to enter your door." Finally the son lost his temper. He struck his old father. I tell you, friends, this rum business takes the humanity out of people—he struck his old father in the face. The father turned to him without the least anger. He said, "My son, you can strike me if you will; you can kill lire if you will, but no man shall enter your public-house unless he goes over my dead body."

Men, listen! No man or woman here tonight will ever enter hell unless by going over the dead body of Jesus Christ. No man or woman here tonight can go out of this place refusing Christ, persisting in sin, without trampling underfoot the form of Him who was crucified on the cross of Calvary for you.

God has piled the obstacles so high in His patient love! Don't try to surmount them tonight. Turn back. Turn out of the path of sin, turn into the path of faith in Jesus Christ. Turn now!

9

The Most Effective Method of Soul-Winning

AT THE PODIUM

R. A. Torrey was one of the most successful mass evangelists in history. Standing at the front of the room in a double-breasted suit and orating with a booming voice, he preached the gospel to huge audiences. He coordinated advertising and cultivated media coverage; his revivals were citywide events. So it is remarkable that from his vantage point in front of huge crowds, he was able to discern that the future of evangelism did not belong to the lone speaker commanding a large audience. Instead, he consistently pointed to personal, peer-to-peer evangelism carried out by all the members of the church as "the most effective method of soul-winning." In later years he would retire from full-time platform speaking in order to focus on training laypeople in evangelism. But this sermon shows that even during his world tour, he was already teaching that a church filled with personal evangelists was far more powerful than even the loudest or most famous visiting evangelist.

Source: R. A. Torrey. *Real Salvation and Whole-Hearted Service*. New York: Revell, 1905, 233–46.

He first findeth his own brother Simon . . . And he brought him to Jesus"—John 1:41–42. The one who brought his brother to Jesus in this passage was Andrew. We are not told that Andrew ever preached a sermon in his life. If he did, the Holy Spirit did not think it was worth putting on record; but his brother, whom he brought to Jesus, preached a sermon that led 3,000 people to Jesus in one day.

Where would Simon Peter's sermon have been if it had not been for Andrew's personal work? The most important kind of Christian work in the world is personal work. We look at the men who stand on the platform and speak to great crowds; but I believe God pays more attention to the man who sits down with a single soul.

A blind woman once came to my office in Chicago and said, "You don't think my blindness will keep me from doing Christian work, do you?"

"No," I replied. "On the contrary, I think it might be a great help to you. A great many people, seeing your blindness, will come and sit down with you, and you can talk with them about the Savior."

"That is not what I mean. I don't want to talk to one person. When a woman can talk to 500 or 600, she don't want to spend time talking to one."

"Your Master could talk to 5,000 at once, for we have it on record, and He did not think it beneath dignity to talk to one at a time."

The Power of Personal Work

Have you ever thought of the tremendous power that there is in personal, hand-to-hand work? One day a man in Boston had in his Sunday school class a boy fresh from the country. He was a very dull boy, and he knew almost nothing about the Bible. He did not even know where to look to find the Gospel of John. He was very much put out because the other boys were bright boys and knew their Bibles. He was just a green country boy, seventeen years of age; but that Sunday school teacher had a heart full of love for Christ and perishing souls.

So one day he went down into the boot shop where that boy worked and said "Would you not like to be a Christian?" The boy had never been approached that way before. Nobody had ever spoken to him about his soul. He said, "Yes; I would like to be a Christian." And that Sunday school teacher explained what it meant to be a Christian, and then he said, "Let us pray."

They knelt down in the back of that boot shop, and the boy, as far as he knew, became a Christian. That boy was Dwight L. Moody. If it had not been for Edward Kimball's faithful, personal work, where would Dwight L. Moody and his great work throughout the world have been?

Probably there are some Sunday school teachers here who say, "I wish I could get down to the great meeting in the big hall; but I have to stay here just teaching a lot of little boys or girls." Who knows who there is in that little class of yours? Who knows what your ignorant little ragged boy may become? Every teacher, make up your mind, by God's help, you will at least make an honest effort to lead everybody in your Sunday school class to Christ today. This world will never be saved by preaching, but this world could soon be evangelized by personal work.

Let us suppose there are 2,000 people in this audience this morning; suppose every one of you became a personal worker, and suppose, by your very best effort, you only succeeded in leading one to Christ in a year, and that one led one to Christ the next year, and so on, what would be the result ? At the end of the year there would be 4,000, at the end of two years there would be 8,000, at the end of three years 16,000, at the end of four years 32,000, at the end of five years 64,000, at the end of six years 128,000, and at the end of seven years 256,000. At the end of eight years your whole city would be won for Christ. At the end of thirty-five years every man, woman, and child on the face of the earth would have heard the Gospel. There is not one that cannot lead at least one to Christ this year. You can instruct every one that you lead to Christ to go out and be a soul-winner. After you get hold of them, send them out, when converted, to lead others, and he bringing one, and that one bringing in another, you will soon touch the whole city.

Why Do Personal Evangelism?
1. Anyone Can Do It

I want to talk about the advantages of personal work.

The first advantage is *anybody can do it*. You cannot all preach. I am glad you can't. What an institution this world would be if we were all preachers! You cannot all sing like Alexander. I am glad you can't, for if you could he would be no curiosity, and you would not come out to hear him sing and give me a chance to preach to you. You can't all even teach Sunday school classes. Some people have an idea that any converted person can teach a Sunday school class. I don't believe it. I think we are making a great mistake in this respect in setting unqualified persons to teaching in Sunday schools; but there is not a child of God who cannot do personal work. A mother with a large family knows she is not called to be a preacher (at least I hope she does), but she can do personal work better than anybody else.

A lady came to me one time—she had five children—and said (I think she had been reading the life of Frances Willard), "I wish I could do some work like that for Christ." I said, "You can work for Christ among all the people you move among." I watched that woman. Every one of her children was brought to Christ—every one! Every woman who came to work in that home was dealt with about her soul. Every butcher's boy or grocer's boy who came around to the door was dealt with about his soul. Every time she went out shopping, she made it a point to talk with the man or woman behind the counter. And when, one dark day, death came into that home and took away a sweet little child, she did not forget to speak to the undertaker, that came to do the last offices for the dead, about his soul. He told me that nothing had ever impressed him in his life as that woman, in the midst of her sorrow, being interested in his soul.

An invalid can do personal work. I have a friend in New York City who has left a life of wealth and fashion to go out to work among the outcast. One day she got hold of a poor outcast girl. She did not live much more than a year after that lady had led her to Christ. She took her to her home to die. As Delia was dying, she wrote to her friends, some in Sing Sing prison, some in the Tombs of New York City—all her friends were among the criminal class—about Christ. Those who were not behind prison bars, she invited to come and see her. My friend told me, "There was a constant procession up the stairway of outcast women and men who come to see Delia, and before Delia died, I knew of one hundred of the most hopeless men and women in New York City that she had led to Christ." That puts us to shame!

Suppose God kindled a fire right here in your hearts, and that you received the anointing of the Spirit of Christ, and every one of you should start out to do personal work. You would not need any evangelist to come from abroad. That is what we have come for, to stir you up to do it.

2. A Person Can Evangelize in Any Place

The second advantage is *you can do it in any place.* You cannot preach in every place. You can preach in the churches two or three times a week; you can preach in the town hall occasionally; you can preach in the streets sometimes. But you cannot go down in the factories and preach often, you cannot go there and hold services; but you can go there and do personal work, if you just hire out there. One man came to our meetings in Liverpool from Hudson's dry soap factory, and he was converted, and every once in a while I get a letter telling me of their meetings there, and now they have a meeting that they conduct outside the building somewhere. In Bradley's foundry a workman got a card to the meetings, and he could not come, so he handed it over to the wickedest man in the shop; that man was grateful for the invitation, thought he would appreciate it by going and was converted at the very first meeting, and went back and told his companions, and there was a revival in the foundry. A telegraph messenger boy was converted in Manchester, and before we were through, there were seventy messenger boys converted in Manchester. There is not a hotel, or a factory, or a public-house where you cannot do personal work.

3. A Person Can Evangelize Anytime

The third advantage is *you can do it at any time.* Any hour of the night, 365 days in the year. Certainly you cannot preach every hour of the day. If you preach three times a day, you are doing well; but there is not an hour of the day or night, between twelve one night and twelve the next night, that you cannot do personal work. You can go out on the streets at night and find the poor wanderers. When I lived in Minneapolis, I employed a missionary just to go out on the streets at night, to speak to the drunkards, outcast women, and night workers, and some of the best conversions were among these people. She had been an outcast herself at one time and was leading them to the Christ that she had found.

Soon after Mr. Moody was converted, he made up his mind that he would not let a day go by without speaking to someone about his soul. One night he came home late—it was nearly ten o'clock. He said, "Here, I haven't spoken to my man today. I guess have lost my chance." He saw a man standing under the lamplight and said to himself, "There's my last chance." He hurried up to him and said, "Are you a Christian?"

"It's none of your business, and if you were not a sort of preacher, I would knock you into the gutter."

"Well," Mr. Moody said, "I just wanted to lead you to Christ."

The next day he went to a friend of Mr. Moody's and said, "That man Moody has got zeal without knowledge. He spoke to me in the street last night, and asked me if I was a Christian. It is none of his business. If he had not been a sort of preacher, I would have knocked him down. He has got zeal without knowledge. He is doing more harm than good."

This friend of Mr. Moody's came to him and said, "See here, Moody, it is all right to be in earnest; but you have got zeal without knowledge. You are doing more harm than good." (Let me say here, it is better to have zeal without knowledge than knowledge without zeal.) Mr. Moody went out, feeling rather cheap and crestfallen. A few weeks passed, and one night there was an awful pounding at his door. Mr. Moody got up and opened the door, and there was this very man. He said, "Mr. Moody, I have not had a night's peace since you spoke to me that night under the lamppost. I have come to ask you to show me how to be a Christian."

Mr. Moody took him in and showed him the way of life, and when the Civil War broke out, that man went and laid down his life for his country.

Another time the thought came to him after he was in bed, "You have not spoken to your man today." But he said, "I am in bed. I cannot get up and go out now." But he could not rest, so he got up and went and opened the door, and it was pouring. "Well," he said, "there is no use going out on the street this awful night. There won't be a soul out in this pouring rain." Just then he heard the patter of a man's feet and saw a man coming. As he came up, Mr. Moody rushed out and said, "Can I have the shelter of your umbrella?" "Certainly." "Have you got a shelter in the time of storm?" and he pointed him to Jesus.

4. Personal Evangelism Can Reach All Classes

The fourth advantage is that *it reaches all classes.* There are a great many people who cannot be reached in any other way than by personal work. Thousands of people could not come to church if they would and thousands would not come to church if they could. This is a splendid hall, just adapted for our purpose and will hold about 10,000 women this afternoon, and 10,000 men tonight; that is 20,000 people inside, and there will be 580,000 outside. It is the 580 that we are after. You cannot reach them by the church, you cannot reach them by the open-air meeting, you cannot reach them by rescue missions. There is only one way you can reach them, and that is by personal work. There is not a man, woman, or child that you cannot reach by personal work. You can reach the policemen, the tramcar men, the railway men, and there is not anybody you cannot reach by personal work.

5. Personal Evangelism Will Hit the Mark

The fifth advantage is that *it hits the mark*. In preaching you have to be more or less general. In personal work you have just one man, just one woman, to talk to, and you can hit the mark every time. You have heard of Henry Ward Beecher. He went out with his father one day, shooting. He had often gone before, but he had never shot anything in his life. Way down yonder was a squirrel. His father said, "Henry, do you see that squirrel?" "Yes, Father." "Would you like to hit it?" "Yes, Father, but I never hit anything in my life."

"You lay the barrel of your gun across the top rail down here and," he continued, "look right down along the barrel. Henry, do you see the squirrel?"

"Yes, Father."

"Well, pull the trigger."

He pulled the trigger, and the squirrel fell at the first shot. The first thing he ever shot in his life. Why? Because it was the first thing he had ever aimed at. That is the trouble with a good deal of our preaching: we aim at nothing and hit it every time.

This is the advantage of personal work: we aim at one definite person. But in our preaching, as Mr. Moody used to say, "I speak to this lady on the front seat, and she passes it over her shoulder to the man back of her, and he passes it to the woman back of him, and she passes it to the man back of her, and they keep passing it on till they pass it out the back door." We have a wonderful power of applying the good points of a sermon to somebody else. When it comes to personal work, there is nobody else to apply it to. I try to be personal in my preaching; but, be just as personal as you can, and yet you will miss your mark.

A man came to my church one morning, a man who was all the time talking about "the deeper life," and had not got an ordinary, decent, everyday kind of Christian life. He had all the phraseology of the deepest Christian experience; a man that talked about being filled with the Spirit and cheated other people in business. I saw him coming into the audience, and I said to myself, "I am glad you have come. I will hit you this morning. I have a sermon just adapted to you."

While I was preaching I would look right at him; so he would know I meant him, and he sat there, beaming up at me. When the sermon was over he came down to me, rubbing his hands. "Oh," he said, "Brother Torrey, I came eight miles to hear you this morning. I have so enjoyed it." That was just what I did not want. I wanted to make him miserable. But I had him now face-to-face, and he did not enjoy it.

That is the advantage of personal work. You can aim right square at the mark and hit it. A man can listen to preaching all day, but he will say, "I don't like this personal work." It hits too hard. He doesn't like to have a person come up and say, "Are you a Christian?" The minister can preach all he pleases, but when he looks you right in the eye, you know it means you. It aims right straight at the mark and hits it.

6. Personal Evangelism Is Effective

The sixth advantage is that *it is effective*. Personal work succeeds where every other kind of work fails. I don't care who the preacher is or how good a preacher he may be; a man or woman who has not been affected by the sermon will be reached by some very ordinary person with the love of God and of souls in his heart. Take Mr. Moody, for example. I think Mr. Moody was as good a preacher as I ever heard. I would rather hear Mr. Moody preach a sermon that I had heard a dozen times than to hear any other man preach a sermon; but as good a preacher as Mr. Moody was, thousands of people would go out utterly unmoved by his sermons. I have seen very ordinary working people, uneducated people, but people who had the love of Christ and of souls in their heart, get hold of the man or woman who had gone out of Mr. Moody's meeting utterly untouched, and in ten or fifteen minutes lead them to the Lord Jesus Christ.

7. Personal Evangelism Can Meet Every Need

The seventh advantage is that *it meets the specific need and every need of the individual*. Even when a man comes to Christ, he has difficulties and doubts, and troubles and questions. He cannot ask them of the preacher. How often a man sits down in the audience and says, "I wish I could speak to that preacher alone." In this personal, hand-to-hand work, a person can ask all the questions he wants to, and you can meet all his difficulties. I am getting letters from people all over the world who have difficulties. My father used to tell a story about a physician in the village who had a jug, and he took a little of every kind of medicine he had in his shop and put it in that jug and shook it up. When anyone came to him and he did not know just what was the matter with them, he would give them a spoonful out of that jug, thinking, "There is something in it that will meet their case, anyhow." That is the way we do in our preaching; we take a little comfort and put it in the sermon, a little bit of conviction, a little bit to show the way of life, and shake it all up and give it to the people. If I were going to be doctored, I would want the doctor to find out my specific difficulty, and I would want to take the kind of medicine that met my specific need. In personal work you give specific passages of Scripture for specific difficulties.

8. Personal Evangelism Produces Abundant Results

The eighth advantage is that *it produces abundant results.* The great services, where the ministers speak to 500, or 1,000, or 5,000, do not produce as abundant results. Suppose a man was pastor of a church of one hundred members, and suppose he was a very faithful minister, and that as a result of his preaching, there were added fifty to his church each year on confession of faith. That would be a pretty good record. In the report of the Presbyterian Churches of America, there were only 200 of the 7,000 that reported over fifty accessions for the year. But suppose by his faithful preaching, this pastor added fifty a year. Now suppose that pastor said, "I am going to train my people to do personal work," and trained his people to do personal work, and suppose only one-half of them would consent to do it. Suppose that these fifty trained workers only succeeded in winning one a month apiece to Christ. That would mean 600 a year. Preaching is not in it with personal work.

But, friends, some of us think we pay the minister to do the work. Your minister is your leader, but you are supposed to work under his leadership. One reason why the church of which I am pastor always has a revival is because the people are trained to do personal work. It has had a revival ever since I have been pastor of it. I have been pastor ten years. There have been ten years of revival. There has never been a month that we have not received new members. There has never been a Sabbath without conversions. We would not know what to make of it if there were a Sabbath without conversions. I do not think there has been any day in the week of all this time—365 days in all—that someone has not been won to

Christ in or about the building. There will be a good many people converted there today. You say, "Who is going to preach?" I don't know. But whoever preaches, there will be conversions, and in the Sabbath school this afternoon, there will be conversions, and in the evening meeting tonight. Why? Because I have a church that believes in and does personal work. Every Sunday evening while I preach, I know there is someone right near everyone in that church who knows how to lead a soul to Christ. There are workers in every section of the church. If anybody gets up and goes out, I like it in Chicago, because just as sure as anybody gets up and leaves, I know that there is at least one person that is going to be spoken to that night. Someone will drop down the stairs behind them, perhaps follow them a block or two before they speak to them.

Go out to the people and ask God to give you power. The Holy Spirit is for every one of us. I do thank God that the great gift of the Son is for the whole world, and that the gift of the Holy Ghost is for every saved one. "If ye then, being evil, know how to give good gifts unto your children: how much more shall your heavenly Father give the Holy Spirit to them that ask him?" (Luke 11:13). Just ask and then go out. Of course, you need to know something about your Bibles in order to do personal work, but you only need one text to start with.

When Mr. Moody first came to New Haven, we thought we would go out and hear this strange, uneducated man. I was in the senior class in the theological department of the university and was just about to take my BD degree. I knew more then than I will ever know in my life again. We thought we would patronize Mr. Moody a little bit. He did not seem at all honored by our presence, and, as we heard that untutored man, we thought, "He may be uneducated, but he knows some things we don't." Some of us had sense enough to go to him and say, "Mr. Moody, we wish you would tell us how to do it." And he told us to come round early the next night and he would tell us, and we theologues went up to the meeting, and he said a few words to us, gave us a few texts of Scripture, and then said, "*You go at it.*" The best way to learn how to do it is to do it.

"He that *goeth forth* and weepeth, bearing precious seed, shall doubtless come again with rejoicing, bringing his sheaves with him" (Psalm 126:6, emphasis added). If, however, you make a stupid blunder the first time, go at it again. But if you never start until you are sure you will not make a blunder, you will make the biggest blunder of your life. Go alone with God first, and see if you are right with God. Put away every known sin out of your life, surrender absolutely to God, ask for the Holy Spirit, and then pitch in.

PART 3

THE BIOLA YEARS AND AFTER

INTRODUCTION

Architect of Radical Evangelicalism

The great years of worldwide revival swept through Torrey's life like a storm. After returning to the United States, Torrey founded a retreat center, conducted a number of American revivals, and took a few more trips abroad to preach. But the great movement was over, and after a few years Torrey settled down to the normal business of his life as a preacher, teacher, and writer.

One thing he had learned from the great revival, however, was that preaching the simple Gospel message was enough. As the increasingly faddish twentieth century rolled along, Torrey would consistently refuse to indulge in spectacle or entertainment just to draw a crowd. He resisted the temptation to recapture the large numbers of his golden days by any means necessary. Instead, he drew this lesson:

> The real Gospel, when preached in the power of the Holy Spirit, produces the same effects in individual lives today, and in the transformation of families and communities, that it has produced throughout all the centuries since our Lord Jesus Christ died on the Cross of Calvary and

> rose again and ascended to the right hand of the Father and poured out His Holy Spirit upon His people. Practical results prove that that Gospel does not even need to be restated, though of course it is desirable to adapt the illustrations and method of argument to the thinking of our own day.[1]

"Practical results prove": Torrey had seen it happen around the world, and he knew his task was to keep at preaching the real Gospel as unadorned as possible. In "The Great Attraction" (chapter 11), he would declare, "Nineteen centuries of Christian history prove the drawing power of Jesus when He is properly presented to men. I have seen some wonderful verification of the assertion of our text as to the marvelous drawing power of the uplifted Christ." He would provide numbers and credentials when necessary, citing the 12,000 who filled Royal Albert Hall (including 2,000 in its dome; see page 168).

R. A. Torrey is one of the founding fathers of conservative evangelicalism. George Marsden has rightly called Torrey "one of the principal architects of fundamentalist thought," though we need to bear in mind that "fundamentalism" came to take on other meanings after the death of R. A. Torrey. We would do well to remember the nineteenth-century origins of those institutions that originally brought forth the conservative evangelical movement for reaffirming fundamentals. Torrey was, after all, a nineteenth-century man. He lived two and a half decades into the twentieth, but he was formed long before that. Even to see him in a photo from 1924, standing in Los Angeles in his double-breasted suit, is to catch sight of a New England Victorian squinting under palm trees in the wrong century. Taking a view from the nineteenth century, Torrey was a fundamentalist; in fact, he and his colaborers invented fundamentalism as a response to the creeping liberalism of the mainline denominations in the early twentieth century. They formed the interdenominational antimodernist coalition that contributed to *The Fundamentals,* a series of twelve small books widely distributed in the second decade of the twentieth century. R. A. Torrey was the final editor of that series, which was financed by oil magnate Lyman Stewart and his brother Milton.

Lyman Stewart had begun investing heavily in founding a Bible institute in Los Angeles (later referred to as BIOLA). Collaborating with his friend T. C. Horton, Stewart planned to replicate what Moody Bible Institute was accomplishing in Chicago. What better way to replicate Moody's success than to hire the man who had been deputized by Moody himself to run the flagship Bible institute? So Stewart and Horton invited R. A. Torrey to come to BIOLA[2] in 1912, and he answered the call, spending twelve years as the figurehead and dominant intellectual force on campus. One of the conditions of his hire was that BIOLA would enable him to start a nondenominational congregation on the Institute's premises, and this came into being as the Church of the Open Door, with Torrey as pastor. In 1924, Torrey left BIOLA to devote time to other ministry opportunities in what would turn out to be the last four years of his life. He died in 1928 and was buried on the grounds of the Montrose retreat center that he founded in Pennsylvania.

R. A. Torrey had been the perfect dean for BIOLA. He combined in one person the academic accomplishment necessary for the head of an educational institution with the passion for evangelism and Christian work that kept this unique place from being just another college or seminary. Any student of BIOLA could point to their dean and say that he embodied the very virtues they came to the school to cultivate. When Torrey departed, Horton and the other leaders (Stewart had already died in 1923) faced the intractable problem of who could replace him. As it turned out, nobody could. They tried unsuccessfully a few times, and ultimately decided that the many things Torrey achieved and symbolized for the school would in the future have to be split among several leaders.

We could say the age of Torreys has passed, and we could lament how our sorry, post-Torrey era is one in which it is impossible to find an intellectual soul-winner or an evangelistic scholar. We could say, as people said after the death of Dwight Moody, that the golden days are behind us and all that's left is maintenance and cleanup operations. But several other possibilities are also open to us as descendants of R. A. Torrey. We could pray that better things are still to come. We could also recognize that, having circled the globe in an epochal revival ministry, R. A. Torrey chose to spend his final season of productive labor investing in training ordinary, nonprofessional Christians in Bible knowledge and personal evangelism.

The right way to carry on the legacy of R. A. Torrey is not to wait for the next big stadium evangelist but to invest in churches, schools, and ministries that know how to train laypeople in doing the work of ministry. Remember that Torrey's plan was to train a much larger team of people to carry on the work that was too great for any one person. The work of R. A. Torrey goes on in places where an army of godly laypeople are being equipped for the work of ministry, united in gratitude, bonded in love, trusting God, obeying Christ, happy in Jesus—corny and nineteenth century as it may sound—and fully surrendered to the Holy Spirit.

Notes

1. R. A. Torrey, *The Gospel for Today* (New York: Revell, 1922), 2.
2. Known then as the Bible Institute of Los Angeles, the school grew through the years and today is Biola University, located in La Mirada, California, a Los Angeles suburb.

10

Walking as Jesus Walked

AT THE PODIUM

As opposed to the sermons from the revival period, this sermon gives us a chance to hear how Torrey preached in his own church during ordinary congregational ministry. In this case, he is preaching in the Church of the Open Door, the interdenominational church that was associated with the Bible Institute of Los Angeles, and of which he was the founding pastor. What it reveals is that Torrey is able to integrate a large number of theological themes into what is essentially a very practical sermon. Here he offers his own interpretation of the "What Would Jesus Do" motto, giving a far more explicitly Trinitarian answer than is normally given to that question. Torrey also balances the theme of Jesus as our Savior with the theme of Jesus as our pattern for imitation, as well as salvation by faith with the demand for good works.

Source: R. A. Torrey. "Walking as Jesus Walked." *The Voice of God in the Present Hour.* New York: Revell, 1917, 231–42.

The one great secret of a life full of blessedness is abiding in Christ. Abiding in Christ is the one all-inclusive secret of power in prayer: our Lord Jesus says in John 15:7, "If ye abide in me, and my words abide in you, ye shall ask what ye will, and it shall be done unto you."

Abiding in Christ is also the secret of fruitfulness. Our Lord Jesus says, "I am the vine, ye are the branches: He that abideth in me, and I in him, the same bringeth forth much fruit: for without me ye can do nothing" (v. 5).

Abiding in Christ is the secret of fullness of joy: in the same chapter to which we have referred twice, the Lord Jesus says, "These things have I spoken unto you [i.e., these things about abiding in Him], that my joy might remain in you, and that your joy might be made full" (v. 11), a clear statement that our joy is made full, or filled full, when we abide in Him alone.

But according to our text this morning, the one proof that we do abide in Him is that we "walk, even as he walked" (1 John 2:6). The great test of whether we are abiding in Christ or not is not some ecstatic feeling but our daily conduct. If we walk as He walked, that is proof, conclusive proof, that we are abiding in Him whether we have ecstatic feelings or not. On the other hand if we do not walk as He walked, that is conclusive proof that we are not abiding in Him, no matter how many ecstasies and raptures we may boast of. So the practical question that faces each one of us this morning is, Am I walking as Jesus walked? This brings us face-to-face with the question, How did Jesus walk?

How Jesus Walked:
1. With a Focus on the Glory of God

Some years ago Charles Sheldon wrote a book named *In His Steps,* in which he tried to imagine how Jesus would act in various imaginary relations of life; how, for example, He would conduct a newspaper, etc. The book awakened a great deal of interest, but was necessarily not very satisfactory. We are not left to our own imaginations in this matter. Far more practical than the question of what Jesus would do in various imaginary relations of life is to find what

He actually did when He was here on earth, and find out how He really walked. How did Jesus walk?

First of all, *He walked with an eye absolutely single to the glory of God.* He says in John 8:50, "I seek not mine own glory." In no act of His whole life did He have regard to His own honor or glory. He was entirely absorbed in the glory of Him who sent Him. In the prayer that He offered the night before His crucifixion, He said, "Father, the hour is come; glorify thy Son" (John 17:1). Now that looks at the first glance as if He were seeking His own glory, but listen to the rest of the petition: "that thy Son also may glorify thee." It was not His own glory that He was seeking but altogether the Father's, and He simply asked the Father to glorify Him that the Father Himself might be glorified. In the fourth verse of the same chapter, we hear Him saying, "I glorified thee on the earth [having accomplished] the work which thou gavest me to do." His own glory was a matter about which He was entirely unconcerned; the glory of the Father was the one thing that absorbed Him. In every act of His life, small or great, He was simply seeking the glory of God. He had an eye absolutely single to the glory of God.

Even in the eternal world before He became incarnate, when He was existing in the form of God, when the whole angelic world saw by His outward form that He was a divine person, and when He might have retained that divine glory, Jesus thought it not a thing to be grasped to be on an equality with God but emptied Himself and "took upon him the form of a servant, and was made in the likeness of men: And being found in fashion as a man he humbled himself, and became obedient unto death, even the death of the cross" (Philippians 2:7–8), because by this giving up His own divine glory and taking upon Himself humility and shame, greater glory would come to the Father.

And now may I put the question to you, and to myself as I put it to you: Are you walking with an eye absolutely single to the glory of God? Is there but one thing that concerns you in determining upon any course of action, viz., will I glorify the Father more by doing this than by not doing it? I heard two Christian women discussing the other day the relative merits of the East and West as a place to live. One spoke about the maples and the oaks and the beeches of the East, about the various social and other advantages. The other dwelt upon the fruits and flowers of Southern California, upon the air and the cleanliness. But if we are to walk as Jesus walked, we will not determine our home by such considerations as these, the whole question will be: Will it be more to God's glory for me to live in the East or the West?

2. In Full Surrender to the Father's Will

Second, a study of the walk of Jesus as recorded in the four Gospels shows us *He walked in wholehearted surrender to and delight in the will of the Father*. Not only could He say, "I do always the things that are pleasing to him," but He even went so far as to say, "My meat," i.e., His sustenance and delight, "is to do the will of him that sent me, and to accomplish his work" (John 4:34 RV). The circumstances under which He said this were significant; He was tired, hungry, and thirsty, so tired that when His disciples went into the neighboring village to buy food for Him and them, He was unable to go along but rested wearily upon the well at Sychar. As he rested there He looked up the road and saw a sinful woman coming toward Him. In His joy in an opportunity of doing the Father's will in winning that lost woman, He entirely forgot His weariness and His hunger, and step-by-step led her to the place where she knew Him as the Christ.

At that moment His disciples again appeared and wondered that He was talking with a woman, and then urged Him to eat of the food that they had brought from the village, saying, "Rabbi, eat." He looked up at them almost in wonder and said, "I have meat to eat that ye know not." In other words, He says, "I am not hungry; I have been eating." The disciples were filled with surprise and said one to another, "Hath any man brought him aught to eat?" Then Jesus answering their thought said, "My meat is to do the will of Him that sent Me, and to accomplish His work" (vv. 31–34 RV). All the joy He asked, all the gratification He asked was an opportunity to do the Father's will. He not only did His Father's will always, but He delighted in doing it, it was His chief gratification, the very sustenance of His innermost being.

Are you walking as Jesus walked? Are you walking in wholehearted surrender to the will of God, studying His Word daily to find out what that will is, doing it every time when you find it, finding your chief delight in doing the will of the Father, no matter how disagreeable in itself that will may be? This is the way Jesus walked. Are you walking as He walked?

3. In Utter Disregard of Self

Third, *He walked in utter disregard of self.* This is involved in what we have already said, but we mention it separately in order to make it clear. His own interests, His own ease, His own comfort, His own honor, His own anything were nothing to Him. "Though he was rich, yet for your sakes he became poor, that ye through his poverty might be rich" (2 Corinthians 8:9). Not His own interests but those of others were His sole consideration. What riches did He give up? The greatest that anyone ever knew; all the possessions and glory of God. How poor did He become? The poorest man the world ever saw. He not only became a man, taking all a man's dishonor upon Himself, He also became a poor man, a despised man. When He went out of this world, He went out of it stripped of everything. He had not had food for many long hours; every shred of clothing was torn from Him as they nailed Him to the cross. He was stripped of all honor and respect, lifted up on the cross as a condemned felon, while jeering mobs passed by mocking Him—and this end He Himself chose because by thus emptying Himself of everything, He secured eternal life and an inheritance incorruptible, undefiled, and that passes not away, for others. His own interests were nothing, the interests of others were everything.

Are you walking as Jesus walked? Are you living your life day by day in utter disregard of your own interests, your own reputation, your own authority, your own comfort, your own honor, doing the things that will bring blessing to others, no matter what loss and dishonor the doing of them may bring to you? "He that saith he abideth in him ought himself also so to walk, even as he walked" (1 John 2:6).

4. With a Consuming Passion for the Lost

Fourth, *He walked with a consuming passion for the salvation of the lost.* He Himself has defined the whole purpose of His coming into this world; in Luke 19:10 He says, "The Son of man is come to seek and to save that which was lost." He had just one purpose in leaving heaven and all its glory and coming down to earth with all its shame, that was the seeking out and saving of the lost. The saving of the lost was the consuming passion of His life. For this He came, for this He lived, for this He prayed, for this He worked, for this He suffered, for this He died.

Are you walking with such a consuming passion for the salvation of the lost? Oh, how many are there of us who indeed are doing something for the salvation of the lost, but what we do is perfunctory; we do it simply because we think it is the thing we ought to do, not because there is a consuming passion within that will not let us rest without doing everything in our power to save the lost, to bring the lost to a saving knowledge of Jesus Christ. If the professedly Christian men and women walked with such a consuming passion for the salvation of the lost as Jesus walked, how long would it be before hundreds and thousands were turning to Christ here in Los Angeles.

5. In a Life of Prayerfulness

Fifth, *He walked in a life of constant prayerfulness*. In Hebrews 5:7 we read that in the days of His flesh He "offered up prayers and supplications with strong crying and tears." His whole life was a life of prayer. The record that we have of His life in the four Gospels is very brief, only eighty-nine very short chapters in all, and yet in this very brief account of the life of our Lord, the words "pray" and "prayer" are used in connection with Him no less than twenty-five times, and His praying is mentioned in places where these words are not used. People wonder what Jesus would do in this relation or that, but the Bible tells us plainly what He actually did do. He prayed. He spent much time in prayer. He would rise a great while before day and go out into the mountain to pray alone. He spent whole nights in prayer. If we are to walk as Jesus walked, we must lead a life of prayerfulness. The man who is not leading a life of prayer, no matter how many excellent things he may be doing, is not walking as Jesus walked.

6. In Diligent Study of the Scriptures

Finally, *He walked in a life characterized by a diligent study of the Word of God*. We see this in many things. His whole thought and the things that He said showed that He was saturated with Old Testament Scripture. He met each one of the three assaults of Satan in His temptation in the wilderness with a quotation from the Old Testament, and we read in Luke 24:27 that "beginning at Moses and all the prophets, he expounded unto them in all the scriptures," conclusively showing that He had pondered long and deep all parts of the Old Testament, the only written Word of God then existing, and in the forty-fourth verse of the same chapter, we read that He said, "All things must be fulfilled, which were written in the law of Moses, and in the prophets, and in the psalms, concerning me." He Himself was the incarnate Word of God; nevertheless, He diligently studied and steeped Himself in the written Word insofar as it then existed. Are you in this matter walking as Jesus walked? Are you digging into the Bible?

Are you saturating yourself with the Word of God? Are you permitting your whole thought and the very language you use to be saturated with Scripture? It was thus that Jesus walked, with an eye absolutely single to the glory of God, in wholehearted surrender to and delight in the will of the Father, in utter disregard of self, with a consuming passion for the salvation of the lost, with a life of constant prayerfulness, in diligent study of the Word of God. Are you thus walking? Many of us doubtless will have to say this morning, "I am not," and that brings us to the next question.

How Can We Walk as Jesus Walked?

How can we walk as Jesus walked? It is a very practical question, and the all-sufficient answer to it is in our text: "He that saith he abideth in him ought himself also so to walk, even as he walked" (1 John 2:6). It is clear from this that there is only one way by which we can walk as He walked, and that is by abiding in Him. But what does that mean?

Our Lord Himself has explained this in John 15:1–5. In these verses He tells us that He is the Vine and we are the branches, and that if we would have fruit and power in prayer, and joy, we must abide in Him, just as the branch that bears fruit must abide in the Vine. That is to say, abiding in Him is maintaining the same relation to Him that a fruitful branch of a grapevine bears to the vine; it has no life of its own, all its life is the inflow of the life of the vine. Its buds and leaves and blossoms and fruit are not its own but simply the outcome of the life of the vine flowing into it and bearing fruit through it. So if we are to abide in Him and bear fruit, we must seek to have no life of our own; we must renounce all our self-efforts after righteousness, not simply renounce our sins but renounce our own thoughts, our own ambitions, our own purposes, our own strength—our own everything—and cast ourselves in utter dependence upon the Lord

Jesus. We are to let Him think His thoughts in us, will His purpose in us, choose His choice through us, work out His own glorious perfection of character in us.

Many try to be like Christ by imitating Christ. It is absolutely impossible for us to imitate Christ in our own strength. The most discouraging thing that any earnest-minded man can attempt is to imitate Christ. Nothing else will plunge a man in deeper despair than to try to imitate Christ in his own strength. Instead of imitating Him, we should open our heart wide for Him to come in and live His own life out through us. Christ in us is the secret of a Christian life.

The only Christ that many professed Christians know is the historic Christ, that is the Christ who lived nineteen centuries ago on this earth and died on the cross of Calvary, an atoning sacrifice for sin. They only know the Christ who died for us on the cross. Oh, we need to know someone further than that if we are to be like Him; we need to know a living Christ today, a Christ who not only arose and ascended to the right hand of the Father but a Christ who has come down and dwells in us, the hope of glory (Colossians 1:27).

From the bottom of my heart, I praise God for Christ for us on the cross. All my hope of acceptance before God is built upon Him bearing my sins in His own body on the cross, and I do praise God for Christ for us. But, oh, how I praise God, not only for Christ for me on the cross but for Christ in me, a living, personal Christ in me today, living His life out through me, and causing me to walk even as Jesus walked. Thus we may have Christ in us. Paul tells us in Galatians 2:20 [RV], "I have been crucified with Christ"; i.e., when Christ was crucified on the cross, He was crucified as our representative and we were crucified in Him. We must see ourselves where God put us on the cross—in the place of death and the curse—and thus cease to live in our own strength. Then he goes on to say,

"It is no longer I that live, but Christ liveth in me"; i.e., as Paul had been crucified with Christ (as he counted himself), what he really was in his standing before God was dead, and as a dead man, no longer seeking to live his own life but letting Jesus Christ live His life out through him. And then he goes on still further to say, "That life which I now live in the flesh I live in faith, the faith which is in the Son of God, who loved me and gave himself for me."

The whole secret of being like Christ is found in these words. We must count self dead; we must give up our self-efforts after likeness to Christ; we must distrust our own strength as much as we distrust our own weakness and our own sin, and instead of striving to live like Christ, let Christ live in us, as He longs to do. Of course we cannot thus have Christ in us until we know Christ for us, making a full atonement for our sins on the cross. Paul explains the whole secret of it in another way in Ephesians 3:16–20. Here he prays for the believers in Ephesus that they "may be strengthened with power through his Spirit in the inward man; that Christ may dwell in your hearts through faith" [RV]. The thought is, it is the work of the Holy Spirit to form an indwelling Christ within us, and the way to know Christ in us is to let the Holy Spirit form Him within us.

Are you walking as Jesus walked? Do you wish to walk as Jesus walked, cost whatever it may? Well then, realize that you have not been walking as Jesus walked, and that the reason you have not walked as Jesus walked is because you have been trying to do it yourself, and give up your own attempts to do it and just look up to the risen Christ, through whose death on the cross, you have found pardon and justification, and let Him come and dwell in you and live His life out through you; to have His perfect will in you, and just trust the Holy Spirit to form this indwelling Christ in your heart.

11

The Great Attraction: The Uplifted Christ

AT THE PODIUM

Another sermon from Torrey's ordinary preaching life in his own church, "The Great Attraction: The Uplifted Christ," shows how Torrey leveraged his credibility as the evangelist who had gone around the world. In this case, he describes his own success at drawing crowds by preaching the Gospel, and then contrasts it with the gimmicks and stunts that were increasingly being used to draw people to churches. He runs the risk of boasting when he repeats the stories of his great success in evangelism. But he stays focused on his main theological point: that Christ Himself is the One who has the power to draw people to Himself.

Source: R. A. Torrey. "The Great Attraction, the Uplifted Christ." *The Gospel for Today*. New York: Revell, 1922, 77–92.

In a recent advertisement of a Sunday evening service in one of our American cities, it was stated that there would be three attractions: a high-class movie show, a popular gospel pianist and his wife, and an aria from the opera *Madame Butterfly*, rendered by a well-known prima donna.

It is somewhat startling when an unusually gifted and popular preacher, or his advertising committee, thinks of the Gospel of the Son of God as having so lost its power to draw that it must be bolstered by putting on a selection from a very questionable opera, rendered by a professional opera singer, as an additional attraction to help out our once crucified and now glorified Savior and Lord.

This advertisement set me to thinking as to what really was the great attraction to men in this day as well as in former days? At once there came to my mind the words of our text containing God's answer to this question: "And I, if I be lifted up from the earth, will draw all men unto myself" (John 12:32 RV). There is nothing else that draws like the uplifted Christ. Nineteen centuries of Christian history prove the drawing power of Jesus when He is properly presented to men. I have seen some wonderful verifications of the assertion of our text as to the marvelous drawing power of the uplifted Christ.

In London, for two continuous months, six afternoons and evenings each week, I saw the great Royal Albert Hall filled and even jammed, and sometimes as many turned away as got in, though it would seat 10,000 people by actual count and stand 2,000 more in the dome. On the opening night of these meetings, a leading reporter of the city of London came to me before the service began and said, "You have taken this building for two consecutive months?"

"Yes."

"And you expect to fill it every day?"

"Yes."

"Why," he said, "no one has ever attempted to hold two weeks' consecutive meetings here of any kind. Gladstone himself could not fill it for two weeks. And you really expect to fill it for two months?"

I replied, "Come and see." He came and he saw.

On the last night, when the place was jammed to its utmost

capacity and thousands outside clamored for admission, he came to me again and I said, "Has it been filled?" He smiled and said, "It has."

But what filled it? No show on earth could have filled it once a day for many consecutive days. The preacher was no remarkable orator. He had no gift of wit and humor and would not have exercised it if he had. The newspapers constantly called attention to the fact that he was no orator, but the crowds came and came and came; rainy days, and fine days they crowded in or stood outside, oftentimes in a downpour of rain, in the vain hope of getting in. What drew them? The uplifted Christ preached and sung in the power of the Holy Ghost, given in answer to the daily prayers of 40,000 people scattered throughout the earth.

In Liverpool, the Tournament Hall, which was said to seat 20,000 people, and that by actual count seated 12,500 comfortably, located several blocks from the nearest streetcar line and perhaps half a mile from all the regular streetcar lines, was filled night after night for three months, and on the last night they crowded 15,000 people into the building at seven o'clock, and then emptied it, and crowded another 15,000 in who had been patiently waiting outside; 30,000 people drawn in a single night!

By what? By whom? Not by the preacher, not by the singer, but by Him who had said nearly nineteen hundred years before, "And I, if I be lifted up from the earth, will draw all men unto myself."

The Exact Meaning of the Text

Let us now look at the exact meaning of the text.

First, notice who the speaker is and the circumstances under which He spoke. The speaker is our Lord Jesus. Not the Christ of men's imaginings but the Christ of reality, the Christ of actual historic fact. Not the Christ of Mary Baker Eddy's maudlin fancy, or of Madam Besant's mystical imaginings, but the Christ of actuality, who lived here among men and was seen, heard, and handled by men, and who was soon to die a real death to save real sinners from a real hell to a real heaven.

The circumstances were these. Certain Greeks among those who went up to worship at the Jewish feast came to one of the apostles, Philip, and said, "We would see Jesus." And Philip went to Andrew and told Andrew what these Greeks said. Andrew and Philip together came and told Jesus. In the heart cry of these Greeks, "We would see Jesus," our Lord recognized the yearning of the universal heart, the heart of Greek, as well as Jew, for a satisfying Savior. The Greeks had their philosophers and sages, their would-be satisfiers and saviors, the greatest the world has ever known: Socrates, Aristotle, Plato, Epictetus, Epimenides, and many others, but they did not save, and they did not satisfy, and the Greeks cried "We would see Jesus"; and in their eager coming Jesus foresaw the millions of all nations who would flock to Him when He had been crucified as the universal Savior, meeting all the needs of all mankind. And so He cried, "And I, if I be lifted up from the earth, will draw all men unto me."

Second, notice the words, "If I be lifted up" (v. 32). To what does Jesus refer? The next verse answers the question. "But this he said, signifying by what manner of death he should die." Jesus referred to His lifting up on the cross, to die as an atoning Savior for all mankind. This verse is often quoted as if it meant that, if we lifted up Christ in our preaching, He would draw men. That is true, and it is a crying shame that we do not hold just *Him* up more in our preaching, and we would draw far more people if we did; but that is not our Lord's meaning. The *lifting* up clearly referred not to His not being lifted up in our preaching but to His lifting up by His enemies on the cross, to expose Him to awful shame and to an agonizing death. It is Christ *crucified* who draws, it is Christ crucified who meets the deepest needs of the heart of all mankind, it is a Savior, a Savior who atones for the sins of men by His death, and thus saves from the holy wrath of an infinitely holy God, who meets the needs of men, and thus draws all men, for all men are sinners. Preach any Christ but a crucified Christ, and you will not draw men for long. Preach any Gospel but a Gospel of atoning blood, and it will not draw for long.

Unitarianism does not draw men. Unitarian churches are born only to die. Their corpses strew New England today. Many of their ministers have been intellectually among the most brilliant our country has ever known, but their churches even under scholarly and brilliant ministers die, die, die. Why? Because Unitarianism presents a Gospel without *atoning blood,* and Jesus has said and history has proven it true, "And I, *if I be lifted up from the earth,* will draw all men unto myself."

"Christian Science," strangely so called, for as has been often truly said, "it is neither Christian nor scientific," draws crowds of men and women of a certain type, men and women who have or imagine that they have physical ailments, and who will follow anything no matter how absurd, that promises them a little surcease from their real or imagined pains. It also draws crowds who wish to fancy that they have some religion without paying the price of true religion, genuine love, real self-sacrifice, and costly sympathy. But Christian Science does not draw all men, that is, all kinds and conditions and ranks of men. No, a bloodless gospel, a gospel with a Christ but not a Christ lifted up on a cross, does not meet the universal needs of men, and so does not draw all men.

Congregationalism of late years has been sadly tinctured with Unitarianism. In spite of the fact that it has been an eyewitness to Unitarianism's steady decay and death, Congregationalism has largely dropped the atoning blood out of its theology, and consequently it is rapidly going to the wall. Its once great Andover Seminary, still great in the size of its endowment that was given for the teaching of Bible orthodoxy, but which the conscienceless teachers of a bloodless theology have deliberately taken for the exploitation of their "damnable heresies" (2 Peter 2:1), and which is still great in the number of its professors, graduated at their annual graduating exercises last spring just three men, one a Japanese, one a Hindu, and one an American. A theology without a crucified Savior, without the atoning blood, won't draw. It does not meet the need. No, no, the words of our Lord are still true, "And I, *if I be lifted up from the earth,* will draw all men unto myself."

Third, notice the words "Draw all men." Does "all men" mean all individuals or men of all races? Did Jesus mean that every man and woman who lived on this earth would be drawn to Him, or did He mean that men of all races would be drawn to Him? The context answers the question. The Greeks, as we have seen, came to one of the apostles, Philip, and said, "We would see Jesus," and Philip had gone and told Andrew, and Andrew and Philip had gone and told Jesus. Our Lord's ministry during His earthly life was to Jews only, and in the coming of these Greeks so soon before His death, our Lord saw the presage of the coming days when by His death on the cross the barrier between Jews and Gentiles would be broken and all nations would have their opportunity equally with the Jews—by His atoning death on the cross men of all nations would be drawn to Him. He did not say that He would draw every individual, but that all races of men, Greeks as well as Jews, Romans, Scythians, French, English, Germans, Japanese, Americans, and men of all nations.

He is a universal Savior, and true Christianity is a universal religion. Islam, Buddhism, Confucianism, and all other religions but Christianity are religions of a restricted application. Christianity, with a crucified Christ as its center, is a universal religion and meets the needs of all mankind. It meets the needs of the European as well as the needs of the Asian, the needs of the Occident as well as the needs of the Orient, the needs of the American Indian and the needs of the African negro; and so our Lord said, "And I, if I be lifted up from the earth, will draw all men unto myself."

No race has ever been found anywhere on this earth to which

the Gospel did not appeal and whose deepest need the crucified Christ did not meet. Many years ago, when Charles Darwin, the eminent English scientist, came in contact with the Terre del Fuegans in their gross degradation, he publicly declared that here was a people to whom it was vain to send missionaries, as the Gospel could not do anything for them. But brave men of God went there and took the Gospel to them in the power of the Holy Spirit, and demonstrated that it met the need of the Terre del Fuegans, with such great results that Charles Darwin publicly admitted his mistake and became a regular subscriber to the work.

The Gospel, with a crucified Christ as its center, meets the needs of all conditions and classes of men as well as of all races. It meets the need of the millionaire and the need of the pauper; it meets the need of great men of science like James D. Dana and Lord Kelvin, and the need of the man or woman who cannot read nor write. It meets the need of the king on the throne and the need of the laborer in the ditch. I myself have seen with my own eyes noblemen and servant girls, university deans and men who could scarcely read, prisoners in penitentiaries and leaders in moral uplift, brilliant lawyers and dull plodding workingmen come under its attraction, and saved by its power. But it was only because I made "*Christ crucified,*" His atoning work, the center of my preaching.

Fourth, notice the words "Unto me." "I . . . will draw all men unto me." The Revised Version reads "Unto *myself,*" and that was just what Jesus said: "And I, if I be lifted up from the earth, will draw all men *unto myself*" (emphasis added). It is not to a creed or a system of doctrine that Jesus draws men but to a Person, to Himself. That is what we need, a *Person,* Jesus Himself. As He Himself once said, "Come *unto me,* all ye that labour and are heavy laden, and I will give you rest" (Matthew 11:28).

Creeds and confessions of faith are all right in their place—they are of great value. The organized church is of great value, it is indispensable, and it is the most important institution in the world today. Society would soon go to rack and ruin without it; we are all under solemn obligation to God and to our fellow man to support the church and belong to it. But creeds and confessions of faith cannot save; the church cannot save. A divine Person *can* save, Jesus Christ, and He alone. So He says, "And I, if I be lifted up from the earth, will draw all men *unto myself*."

Why Christ Lifted Up on the Cross Draws All Men unto Himself

But why does Christ lifted up on the cross, the crucified Christ, draw all men unto Himself? There are two reasons why Christ lifted up, and Christ *crucified* draws all men unto Himself.

First, Christ crucified draws all men unto Himself because Christ crucified meets the first, the deepest, the greatest, and most fundamental need of man. What is man's first, deepest, greatest, most fundamental need? A Savior. A Savior from what? First of all, and underlying all else, a Savior from the guilt of sin. Every man of every race has sinned. As Paul wrote in Romans 3:22–23, "There is no difference: For all have sinned, and come short of the glory of God." There is no difference between Jew and Gentile at this point, nor is there any difference between English and German at this point, there is no difference between American and Japanese, no difference between European and Asian, no difference between the American and the African, "for all have sinned and come short of the glory of God."

Every man of every race is a sinner; "there is no difference" at this point. And every man shall have to answer for his sin to the infinitely holy God who rules this universe. Therefore, all men need an atoning Savior, who can by His atoning death make propitiation for, and so cover up, our sins, and thus reconcile us to this holy God. The Savior will deliver us from His awful wrath, and bring us out into the glorious sunlight of His favor. And Jesus lifted up is the only atoning Savior in the universe. He who alone was at the same time God and man, He alone can make atonement for sin; and He has made it, has made a perfect atonement, and God has accepted His atonement and testified to His acceptance of His atonement by raising Him from the dead.

The Lord Jesus actually meets our need—He meets every man's first, greatest, deepest, most fundamental need, and He alone. In all the universe there is no other religion but Christianity that even offers an atoning Savior. Mohammedanism, [Islam] offers Muhammad, "the prophet"—a teacher, but not a Savior. Buddhism offers Buddha, supposedly at least a wonderful teacher, "The Light of Asia," but not an atoning Savior. Confucianism offers Confucius, a marvelous teacher far ahead of his time, but not an atoning Savior. No religion offers an atoning Savior—offers an atonement of any real character—but Christianity. This is the radical point of difference between Christianity and every other religion in the world, yet some fool preachers are trying to eliminate from Christianity this, its very point of radical difference from all other religions. But such an emasculated Christianity will not reach the needs of men and will not draw men. It never has and it never will.

The Bible and history are at one at this point. Jesus Christ offers Himself lifted up on the cross to redeem us from the curse of the law, by "becoming a curse in our behalf." "Christ hath redeemed us from the curse of the law, being made a curse for us: for it is written, Cursed is every one that hangeth on a tree" (Galatians 3:13). Men know their need; they may try to forget it, they may try to deny it, they may try to drown their sense of it by drink and dissipation or by wild pleasure-seeking or wild money-getting, or by listening to fake preachers in supposedly orthodox pulpits—like one who in this city declared recently that, "the old sense of sin is fast disappearing." He added: "The change is for the better, not for the worse." He spoke also of "imaginary and artificial sins like 'the sin of unbelief,'" and then went on to say, "In this we agree with Christ," apparently not knowing enough about the Bible to know that Jesus Himself was the very one who said in John 16:8–9, "And he, when he is come, will convict the world in respect of sin, and of righteousness, and of judgment; of sin, *because they believe not on me*" (RV, emphasis added).

But in spite of all our attempts to drown or stupefy or silence our sense of sin, our consciousness of guilt before a Holy God, we all have it, and like Banquo's Ghost, it will not drown. Nothing gives the guilty conscience abiding peace but the atoning blood of Jesus Christ. And so, Christ *lifted up* draws all men unto Him, and even wicked ministers of Satan, like the preacher I have just referred to, sometimes come to their senses and flee to the real Christ, *Christ crucified*, as I hope this one may.

Yes, Jesus, Jesus only, Jesus *lifted up on the cross*, Jesus crucified for our sins, making full atonement for our sins, He and He alone meets the deepest need of us all, and so His cross draws us all unto Himself. Happy is the man or the woman who yields to that drawing. Woe be to the man or woman who resists that drawing; final gloom, despondency, and despair are their lot. Oh, how many men and women who have gotten their eyes opened to see the facts, to see their awful guilt, and who have been plunged into deepest consequent despair, have come to me, and I have pointed them to *Jesus on the cross*, and have shown them by God's Word all their sins laid upon Him and thus settled. They have come to Him and believed God's testimony about Him, that He had borne all their sins in His own body on the cross, and they have found perfect peace and boundless joy.

Will you set out to find peace? If you do not, great gloom, utter despair, awaits you some day, in this world or in the world to come. In my first pastorate I tried to get a man to come to *Christ lifted up* to meet his need of pardon; but though it was many years ago, he held to the theology that is preached as "*new* theology" today, and sought to still the voice of conscience, and stupefy his sense of sin by denying his guilt and his need of an atoning Savior. He did not wish to listen to me nor to see me. But the hour came when death drew nigh. A cancer was eating its way into his brain; then he cried to those about his dying bed, "Send for Mr. Torrey."

I hurried to his side. He was in despair. "Oh!" he said, "Dr. Tidhall tells me that I have but a short time to live, that as soon as this cancer gets a little further, I am a dead man. Tell me how to be saved."

I sat down beside him and told him what to do to be saved. I tried to make as plain as I knew how the way of salvation through the *uplifted Christ,* Christ uplifted on the cross, and I think I know how to make it plain, but he had waited too long, he could not grasp it. I stayed with him. Night came on. I said to his family, "You have been up night after night with him; I will sit with him tonight." They instructed me what to do, how to minister to him. Time after time during the night, I had to go to another room to get some nourishment for him, and as I would come back into the room where he lay, from his bed in the corner there would rise the constant cry, "Oh, I wish I were a Christian. Oh, I wish I were a Christian. Oh, I wish I were a Christian." And thus he died.

Second, Christ crucified draws all men unto Him, because lifted up there to die He reveals His wonderful love for us, and the wondrous love of the Father for us. "Hereby perceive we the love of God, because he laid down his life for us" (1 John 3:16), and "God commendeth his love toward us, in that, while we were yet sinners, *Christ died for us*" (Romans 5:8). There is nothing that draws men like love. Love draws all men in every clime. But no other love draws like the love of God. John 3:16 has broken thousands of hard hearts that resist: "For God so loved the world, that he gave his only begotten Son, that whosoever believeth in him should not perish, but have everlasting life."

One night, preaching in my own church in Minneapolis, the whole choir stayed for the after meeting. The leading soprano was an intelligent young woman but living a worldly life. She remained with the rest. In the after meeting her mother arose in the back of the church and said, "I wish you would pray for the conversion of my daughter." I did not look around but knew instinctively that her cheeks were flushing, and her eyes flashing with anger. As soon as the meeting was dismissed, I hurried down so that I would meet her before she got out of the church. As she came toward me I held out my hand to her. She stamped her foot, and with flashing eyes cried, "Mr. Torrey, my mother knows better than to do that. She knows it will only make me worse."

I said, "Sit down, Cora."

She sat down, and without any argument I opened my Bible to Isaiah 53:5, and began to read, "But he was wounded for our transgressions; he was bruised for our iniquities: the chastisement of our peace was upon him; and with his stripes we are healed." She burst into tears, and the next night accepted Jesus Christ.

I had to go to Duluth for a few days, and when I returned I found that she was seriously ill. One morning her brother came hurrying up to my home and said that she was apparently dying, that she was unconscious, and white from the loss of blood. I hastened down, and as I entered the room she lay there with her eyes closed, with the whitest face I ever saw on one who was not actually dead. She was apparently unconscious, scarcely breathing. I knelt by her side to pray, more for the sake of the mother who stood beside the bed than for her, for I supposed that she was beyond help or hearing. But no sooner had I finished my prayer, than in a clear, full, richly musical tone she began to pray.

These were about her words: "Heavenly Father, if it be Your will, raise me up that as I have used my voice for myself and only to please myself, I may use my voice for Your glory, but if in Your wisdom You see that it is best for me not to live, I shall be glad to go to be with Christ," and she went to be with Christ.

Oh, I have seen thousands melted as I have repeated to them and shown them the picture of Christ on the cross, as told in Isaiah

53:5, "But he was wounded for our transgressions; he was bruised for our iniquities: the chastisement of our peace was upon him; and with his stripes we are healed."

A few days ago I received a missionary magazine containing a testimony from one who was going to Egypt under the Egypt General Mission. This young missionary said, "When I was twelve years old, during the Torrey-Alexander meetings, in 1904, I gave my heart to the Lord Jesus Christ. Dr. Torrey was speaking on the text, Isaiah 53:5, and he asked us to repeat the words with him, but changing the word 'our' into the word 'my.' While repeating the text in this way I suddenly realized, as if for the first time, that Jesus had really suffered all this for me, and there and then I gave my life to Him."

Oh, men and women, look now! See Jesus Christ lifted up on the cross, see Him hanging on that awful cross, see Him wounded for your transgressions, bruised for your iniquities, and the chastisement of your peace laid on Him. Oh, men and women living in sin, men and women rejecting Christ for the world, men and women who have looked to the lies of Christian Science, Unitarianism, and other systems that deny His atoning blood, listen! "But he was wounded for our transgressions; he was bruised for our iniquities; the chastisement of our peace was upon him; and with his stripes we are healed." Won't you yield to that love, won't you give up your sin, give up your worldly pleasures, give up your willful errors, and accept the Savior who loves you, and died for you, who was "wounded for your transgressions; bruised for your iniquities" and upon whom the chastisement of your peace was laid? Accept Him right now.

12

Why God Used D. L. Moody

AT THE PODIUM

This is one of Torrey's most famous sermons, reprinted frequently, often as its own stand-alone booklet. In describing the power of Moody in a series of traits that could each be the subject of its own sermon, Torrey seems to be describing the ideal of what an evangelical minister ought to be. In fact, he may be describing himself in certain ways, or at least what he aspired to be. But Torrey was always insistent that he learned all of these characteristics from his discipleship to Dwight Moody, and he considered it a sacred trust to pass along a clear and compelling description of what a minister of the Gospel could be.

Source: R. A. Torrey. *Why God Used D. L. Moody*. New York: Revell, 1923.

My subject is "Why God Used D. L. Moody," and I can think of no subject upon which I would rather speak. For I shall not seek to glorify Mr. Moody but the God who by His grace, His entirely unmerited favor, used him so mightily, and the Christ who saved him by His atoning death and resurrection life, and the Holy Spirit who lived in him and wrought through him and who alone made him the mighty power that he was to this world.

Furthermore, I hope to make it clear that the God who used D. L. Moody in his day is just as ready to use you and me, in this day, if we, on our part, do what D. L. Moody did, which was what made it possible for God to so abundantly use him.

The whole secret of why D. L. Moody was such a mightily used man, you will find in Psalm 62:11: "God hath spoken once; twice have I heard this, that power belongeth unto God." I am glad it does. I am glad that power did not belong to D. L. Moody; I am glad that it did not belong to Charles G. Finney; I am glad that it did not belong to Martin Luther; I am glad that it did not belong to any other Christian man whom God has greatly used in this world's history. Power belongs to God. If D. L. Moody had any power, and he had great power, he got it from God.

But God does not give His power arbitrarily. It is true that He gives it to whomsoever He will, but He wills to give it on certain conditions, which are clearly revealed in His Word, and Dwight L. Moody met those conditions and God made him the most wonderful preacher of his generation; yes, I think the most wonderful man of his generation.

But how was it that Moody had that power of God so wonderfully manifested in his life? Pondering this question, it seems to me that there were seven things in the life of D. L. Moody that accounted for God's using him so largely as He did.

1. A Fully Surrendered Man

The first thing that accounts for God's using D. L. Moody so mightily was that *he was a fully surrendered man*. Every ounce of that 280-pound body of his belonged to God; everything he was and everything he had belonged wholly to God. Now, I am not saying that Mr. Moody was perfect; he was not. If I attempted to, I presume I could point out some defects in his character, some places where he might have been improved. No, Mr. Moody was not a faultless man. If he had any flaws in his character, and he had, I presume I was in a position to know them better than almost any other man, because of my very close association with him in the later years of his life; and, furthermore, I suppose that in his latter days he opened his heart to me more fully than to anyone else in the world. I think he told me some things that he told no one else. I presume I knew whatever defects there were in his character as well as anybody. But while I recognized such flaws, nevertheless, I know that he was a man who belonged wholly to God.

The first month I was in Chicago, we were having a talk about something upon which we very widely differed, and Mr. Moody turned to me very frankly and very kindly and said in defense of his own position: "Torrey, if I believed that God wanted me to jump out of that window, I would jump." I believe he would. If he thought God wanted him to do anything, he would do it. He belonged wholly, unreservedly, entirely to God.

Henry Varley, a very intimate friend of Mr. Moody in the earlier days of his work, loved to tell how he once said to him: "It remains to be seen what God will do with a man who gives himself up wholly to Him." I am told that when Mr. Henry Varley said that, Mr. Moody said to himself, "Well, I will be that man." And I, for my part, do not think "it remains to be seen what God will do with a man who gives himself up wholly to Him." I think it has been seen already in D. L. Moody. If you and I are to be used in our sphere as D. L. Moody was used in his, we must put all that we have and all that we are in the hands of God, for Him to use as He will, to send us where He will, for God to do with us what He will, and we, on our part, to do everything God bids us do.

There are thousands and tens of thousands of men and women in Christian work, brilliant men and women, rarely gifted men and women, men and women who are making great sacrifices, men and women who have put all conscious sin out of their lives, yet who, nevertheless, have stopped short of absolute surrender to God, and therefore have stopped short of fullness of power. But Mr. Moody did not stop short of absolute surrender to God; he was a wholly surrendered man, and if you and I are to be used, you and I must be wholly surrendered men and women.

2. A Man of Prayer

The second reason for the great power exhibited in Mr. Moody's life was that *Mr. Moody was in the deepest and most meaningful sense a man of prayer*. People often say to me, "Well, I went many miles to see and to hear D. L. Moody, and he certainly was a wonderful preacher." Yes, D. L. Moody certainly was a wonderful preacher; taking it all in all, the most wonderful preacher I have ever heard, and it was a great privilege to hear him preach as he alone could preach. But out of a very intimate acquaintance with him, I wish to testify that he was a far greater *prayer* than he was preacher.

Time and time again he was confronted by obstacles that seemed insurmountable, but he always knew the way to surmount and to overcome all difficulties. He knew the way to bring to pass anything that needed to be brought to pass. He knew and believed in the deepest depths of his soul that "nothing was too hard for the Lord" and that prayer could do anything that God could do.

Oftentimes Mr. Moody would write me when he was about to undertake some new work, saying, "I am beginning work in such and such a place on such and such a day; I wish you would get the students together for a day of fasting and prayer," and often I have taken those letters and read them to the students in the lecture room and said, "Mr. Moody wants us to have a day of fasting and prayer, first for God's blessing on our own souls and work, and then for God's blessing on him and his work." Often we were gathered in the lecture room far into the night—sometimes till one, two, three, four, or even five o'clock in the morning, crying to God, just because Mr. Moody urged us to wait upon God until we received His blessing. How many men and women I have known whose lives and characters have been transformed by those nights of prayer and who have wrought mighty things in many lands because of those nights of prayer!

One day Mr. Moody drove up to my house at Northfield and said, "Torrey, I want you to take a ride with me." I got into the carriage and we drove out toward Lover's Lane, talking about some great and unexpected difficulties that had arisen in regard to the work in Northfield and Chicago, and in connection with other work that was very dear to him. As we drove along, some black storm clouds lay ahead of us, and then suddenly, as we were talking, it began to rain. He drove the horse into a shed near the entrance to Lover's Lane to shelter the horse, and then laid the reins upon the dashboard and said, "Torrey, pray," and then, as best I could, I prayed, while he in his heart joined me in prayer. And when my voice was silent, he began to pray. Oh, I wish you could have heard that prayer! I shall never forget it, so simple, so trustful, so definite, and so direct and so mighty.

When the storm was over and we drove back to town, the obstacles had been surmounted, and the work of the schools, and other work that was threatened, went on as it had never gone on before, and it has gone on until this day. As we drove back, Mr. Moody said to me, "Torrey, we will let the other men do the talking and the criticizing, and we will stick to the work that God has given us to do, and let Him take care of the difficulties and answer the criticisms."

On one occasion Mr. Moody said to me in Chicago, "I have just found, to my surprise, that we are twenty thousand dollars behind in our finances for the work here and in Northfield, and we must have that twenty thousand dollars, and I am going to get it by prayer." He did not tell a soul who had the ability to give a penny of the twenty thousand dollars deficit, but looked right to God and said, "I need twenty thousand dollars for my work; send me that money in such a way that I will know it comes straight from You." And God heard that prayer. The money came in such a way that it was clear that it came from God, in direct answer to prayer.

Yes, D. L. Moody was a man who believed in the God who answers prayer, and not only believed in Him in a theoretical way but believed in Him in a practical way. He was a man who met every difficulty that stood in his way—by prayer. Everything he undertook was backed up by prayer, and in everything, his ultimate dependence was upon God.

3. A Deep, Practical Student of the Bible

The third reason why God used D. L. Moody was because *he was a deep and practical student of the Word of God.* Nowadays it is often said of D. L. Moody that he was not a student. I wish to say that he was a student; most emphatically he was a student. He was not a student of psychology, he was not a student of anthropology—I am very sure he would not have known what that word meant—he was not a student of biology, he was not a student of philosophy, he was not even a student of theology, in the technical sense of the term. But he was a student, a profound and practical student of the one Book that is more worth studying than all other books in the world put together: he was a student of the Bible.

Every day of his life, I have reason for believing, he arose very early in the morning to study the Word of God, way down to the close of his life. Mr. Moody used to rise about four o'clock in the morning to study the Bible. He would say to me: "If I am going to get in any study, I have got to get up before the other folks get up," and he would shut himself up in a remote room in his house, alone with his God and his Bible.

I shall never forget the first night I spent in his home. He had invited me to take the superintendency of the Bible Institute and I had already begun my work, was on my way to some city in the East to preside at the International Christian Workers' Convention. He wrote me, saying, "Just as soon as the convention is over, come up to Northfield." He learned when I was likely to arrive and drove over to South Vernon to meet me. That night he had all the teachers from the Mount Hermon School and from the Northfield Seminary come together at the house to meet me, and to talk over the problems of the two schools. We talked together far into the night, and then, after the principals and teachers had gone home, Mr. Moody and I talked together about the problems awhile longer. It was very late when I got to bed that night, but very early the next morning, about five o'clock, I heard a gentle tap on my door. Then I heard Mr. Moody's voice whispering, "Torrey, are you up?" I happened to be; I do not always get up at that early hour, but I happened to be up that particular morning. He said, "I want you to go somewhere with me," and I went down with him. Then I found out that he had already been up an hour or two in his room, studying the Word of God.

Oh, you may talk about power, but if you neglect the one Book that God has given you as the one instrument through which He imparts and exercises His power, you will not have it. You may read many books and go to many conventions and you may have your all-night prayer meetings to pray for the power of the Holy Ghost, but unless you keep in constant and close association with the one book, the Bible, you will not have power. And if you ever had power, you will not maintain it except by the daily, earnest, intense study of that Book. *Ninety-nine Christians in every hundred are merely playing at Bible study; and therefore ninety-nine Christians in every hundred are mere weaklings, when they might be giants, both in their Christian life and in their service.*

It was largely because of his thorough knowledge of the Bible and his practical knowledge of the Bible that Mr. Moody drew such immense crowds. On "Chicago Day," in October 1893, none of the theaters of Chicago dared to open because it was expected that everybody in Chicago would go on that day to the World's Fair, and, in point of fact, something like 400,000 people did pass through the gates of the Fair that day. Everybody in Chicago was expected to be at that end of the city on that day. But Mr. Moody said to me, "Torrey, engage the Central Music Hall and announce meetings from nine o'clock in the morning till six o'clock at night."

"Why," I replied, "Mr. Moody, nobody will be at this end of Chicago on that day; not even the theaters dare to open; everybody is going down to Jackson Park to the Fair; we cannot get anybody out on this day."

Mr. Moody replied, "You do as you are told," and I did as I was told, and engaged the Central Music Hall for continuous meetings from nine o'clock in the morning till six o'clock at night. But I did it with a heavy heart; I thought there would be poor audiences. I was on the program at noon that day. Being very busy in my office about the details of the campaign, I did not reach the Central Music Hall till almost noon. I thought I would have no trouble in getting in. But when I got almost to the hall, I found to my amazement that not only was it packed but the vestibule was packed and the steps were packed, and there was no getting anywhere near the door; and if I had not gone round and climbed in a back window, they would have lost their speaker for that hour. But that would not have been of much importance, for the crowds had not gathered to hear me; it was the magic of Mr. Moody's name that had drawn them.

And why did they long to hear Mr. Moody? Because they knew that while he was not versed in many of the philosophies and fads and fancies of the day, that he did know the one Book that this old world most longs to know—the Bible.

I shall never forget Moody's last visit to Chicago. The ministers of Chicago had sent me to Cincinnati to invite him to come to Chicago and hold a meeting. In response to the invitation, Mr. Moody said to me, "If you will hire the Auditorium for weekday mornings and afternoons and have meetings at ten in the morning and three in the afternoon, I will go."

I replied, "Mr. Moody, you know what a busy city Chicago is, and how impossible it is for businessmen to get out at ten o'clock in the morning and three in the afternoon on working days. Will you not hold evening meetings and meetings on Sunday?"

"No," he replied, "I am afraid if I did, I would interfere with the regular work of the churches."

I went back to Chicago and engaged the Auditorium, which at that time was the building having the largest seating capacity of any building in the city, seating in those days about 7,000 people, and announced weekday meetings with Mr. Moody as the speaker, at ten o'clock in the mornings and three o'clock in the afternoons. At once protests began to pour in upon me. One of them came from Marshall Field, at that time the business king of Chicago. "Mr. Torrey," Mr. Field wrote, "we businessmen of Chicago wish to hear Mr. Moody and you know perfectly well how impossible it is for us to get out at ten o'clock in the morning and three o'clock in the afternoon; have evening meetings."

I received many letters of a similar purport and wrote to Mr. Moody, urging him to give us evening meetings. But Mr. Moody simply replied, "You do as you are told," and I did as I was told; that is the way I kept my job.

On the first morning of the meetings, I went down to the Auditorium about half an hour before the appointed time, but I went with much fear and apprehension; I thought the Auditorium would be nowhere nearly full. When I reached there, to my amazement I found a queue of people four abreast extending from the Congress Street entrance to Wabash Avenue, then a block north on Wabash Avenue, then a break to let traffic through, and then another block, and so on. I went in through the back door, and there were many clamoring for entrance there.

When the doors were opened at the appointed time, we had a cordon of twenty policemen to keep back the crowd, but the crowd was so great that it swept the cordon of policemen off their feet and packed 8,000 people into the building before we could get the doors shut. And I think there were as many left on the outside as there were in the building. I do not think that anyone else in the world could have drawn such a crowd at such a time.

Why? Because though Mr. Moody knew little about science, or philosophy, or literature, in general, he did know the one Book that this old world is perishing to know and longing to know, and this old world will flock to hear men who know the Bible and preach the Bible as they will flock to hear nothing else on earth.

During all the months of the World's Fair in Chicago, no one could draw such crowds as Mr. Moody. Judging by the papers, one would have thought that the great religious event in Chicago at that time was the World's Congress of Religions. One very gifted man of letters in the East was invited to speak at this congress. He saw in this invitation the opportunity of his life and prepared his paper, the exact title of which I do not now recall, but it was something along the line of "New Light on the Old Doctrines." He prepared the paper with great care and then sent it around to his most trusted and gifted friends for criticisms. These men sent it back to him with such emendations as they had to suggest. Then he rewrote the paper, incorporating as many of the suggestions and criticisms as seemed wise. Then he sent it around for further criticisms. Then he wrote the paper a third time and had it, as he trusted, perfect. He went on to Chicago to meet this coveted opportunity of speaking at the World's Congress of Religions. It was at eleven o'clock on a Saturday morning (if I remember correctly) that he was to speak. He stood outside the door of the platform waiting for the great moment to arrive, and as the clock struck eleven he walked onto the platform to face a magnificent audience of eleven women and two men! But there was not a building anywhere in Chicago that would accommodate the very same day the crowds that would flock to hear Mr. Moody at any hour of the day or night.

Oh men and women, if you wish to get an audience and wish

to do that audience some good after you get them, study, study, STUDY the one Book, and preach, preach, PREACH the one Book, and teach, teach, TEACH the one Book, the Bible—the only Book that contains God's Word, and the only Book that has power to gather and hold and bless the crowds for any great length of time.

4. A Humble Man

The fourth reason that God continuously, through so many years, used D. L. Moody was because *he was a humble man*. I think D. L. Moody was the humblest man I ever knew in all my life. He loved to quote the words of another: "Faith gets the most, love works the most, but *humility keeps the most*." He himself had the humility that keeps everything it gets.

As I have already said, he was the most humble man I ever knew, i.e., the most humble man when we bear in mind the great things he did, and the praise that was lavished upon him. How he loved to put himself in the background and put other men in the foreground. How often he would stand on a platform with some of us little fellows seated behind him, and as he spoke he would say, "There are better men coming after me." As he said it, he would point back over his shoulder with his thumb to the "little fellows." I do not know how he could believe it, but he really *did* believe that the others that were coming after him were really better than he was. He made no pretense to a humility he did not possess. In his heart of hearts he constantly underestimated himself and overestimated others. He really believed that God would use other men in a larger measure than he had been used.

Mr. Moody loved to keep himself in the background. At his conventions at Northfield, or anywhere else, he would push the other men to the front and, if he could, have them do all the preaching—McGregor, Campbell Morgan, Andrew Murray, and the rest of them. The only way we could get him to take any part in the program was to get up in the convention and move that we hear D. L. Moody at the next meeting. He continually put himself out of sight.

Oh, how many a man has been full of promise and God has used him, and then the man thought that he was the whole thing and God was compelled to set him aside! I believe more promising workers have gone on the rocks through self-sufficiency and self-esteem than through any other cause. I can look back for forty years, or more, and think of many men who are now wrecks who at one time the world thought were going to be something great. But they have disappeared entirely from the public view. Why? Because of overestimation of self.

I remember a man with whom I was closely associated in a great movement in this country. We were having a most successful convention in Buffalo, and he was greatly elated. As we walked down the street together to one of the meetings one day, he said to me, "Torrey, you and I are the most important men in Christian work in this country" (or words to that effect). I replied, "John, I am sorry to hear you say that; for as I read my Bible I find man after man who had accomplished great things whom God had to set aside because of his sense of his own importance." And God set that man aside also from that time. I think he is still living, but no one ever hears of him and has not heard of him for years.

God used D. L. Moody, I think, beyond any man of his day, but it made no difference how much God used him, he never was puffed up. One day, speaking to me of a great New York preacher, now dead, Mr. Moody said, "He once did a very foolish thing, the most foolish thing that I ever knew a man, ordinarily so wise as he was, to do. He came up to me at the close of a little talk I had given and said, 'Young man, you have made a great address tonight.'" Then Mr. Moody continued, "How foolish of him to have said that; it almost turned my head." But, thank God, it did *not* turn his head, and even when pretty much all the ministers in England, Scotland,

and Ireland, and many of the English bishops were ready to follow D. L. Moody wherever he led, even then it never turned his head one bit. He would get down on his face before God, knowing he was human, and ask God to empty him of all self-sufficiency. And God did.

Oh men and women, especially young men and young women, perhaps God is beginning to use you; very likely people are saying, "What a wonderful gift he has as a Bible teacher, what power he has as a preacher, for such a young man!" Listen: get down upon your face before God. I believe here lies one of the most dangerous snares of the Devil. When the Devil cannot discourage a man, he approaches him on another tack, which he knows is far worse in its results; he puffs him up by whispering in his ear, "You are the leading evangelist of the day. You are the man who will sweep everything before you. You are the coming man. You are the D. L. Moody of the day," and if you listen to him, he will ruin you. The entire shore of the history of Christian workers is strewn with the wrecks of gallant vessels that were full of promise a few years ago, but these men became puffed up and were driven on the rocks by the wild winds of their own raging self-esteem.

5. A Freedom from the Love of Money

The fifth reason God used D. L. Moody was *his entire freedom from the love of money*. Mr. Moody might have been a wealthy man, but money had no charms for him. He loved to gather money for God's work; he refused to accumulate money for himself.

He told me during the World's Fair that if he had taken, for himself, the royalties on the hymnbooks that he had published, they would have amounted, at that time, to a million dollars. But Mr. Moody refused to touch the money. He had a perfect right to take it, for he was responsible for the publication of the books, and it was his money that went into the publication of the first of them. Mr. Sankey had some hymns that he had taken with him to England, and he wished to have them published. He went to a publisher (I think Morgan & Scott), and they declined to publish them, because, as they said, Philip Phillips had recently been over and published a hymnbook and it had not done well. However, Mr. Moody had a little money and he said that he would put it into the publication of these hymns in cheap form and he did. The hymns had a most remarkable and unexpected sale; they were then published in book form and large profits accrued. The financial results were offered to Mr. Moody, but he refused to touch them.

Someone urged him: "But the money belongs to you," but he would not touch it. Mr. Fleming H. Revell was at the time treasurer of the Chicago Avenue Church, commonly known as the Moody Tabernacle. Only the basement of this new church building had been completed, funds having been exhausted. Hearing of the hymnbook situation, Mr. Revell suggested, in a letter to friends in London, that the money be given for completion of this building, and it was. Afterward, so much money came in that it was given, by the committee into whose hands Mr. Moody put the matter, to various Christian enterprises.

In a certain city to which Mr. Moody went in the latter years of his life, and where I went with him, it was publicly announced that Mr. Moody would accept no money whatever for his services. Now, in point of fact, Mr. Moody was dependent, in a measure, upon what was given him at various services, but when this announcement was made, Mr. Moody said nothing, and left that city without a penny's compensation for the hard work he did there and, I think, paid his own hotel bill. And yet a minister in that very city came out with an article in a paper, which I read, in which he told a fairy tale of the financial demands that Mr. Moody made upon them, which story I knew personally to be absolutely untrue. Millions of dollars passed into Mr. Moody's hands, *but they passed through*; they did not stick to his fingers.

The love of money on the part of some evangelists has done

more to discredit evangelistic work in our day, and to lay many an evangelist on the shelf, than almost any other cause. While I was away on my recent tour, I was told by one of the most reliable ministers in one of our eastern cities of a campaign conducted by one who has been greatly used in the past. (Do not imagine, for a moment, that I am speaking of Billy Sunday, for I am not.) This evangelist of whom I now speak came to a city for a united evangelistic campaign and was supported by fifty-three churches. The minister who told me about the matter was himself chairman of the finance committee. The evangelist showed such a longing for money and so deliberately violated the agreement he had made before coming to the city and so insisted upon money being gathered for him in other ways than he had himself prescribed in the original contract, that this minister threatened to resign from the finance committee. He was however persuaded to remain to avoid a scandal.

6. A Consuming Passion for the Salvation of the Lost

The sixth reason God used D. L. Moody was because of *his consuming passion for the salvation of the lost*. Mr. Moody made the resolution, shortly after he himself was saved, that he would never let twenty-four hours pass over his head without speaking to at least one person about his soul. His was a very busy life, and sometimes he would forget his resolution until the last hour, and sometimes he would get out of bed, dress, go out, and talk to someone about his soul in order that he might not let one day pass without having definitely told at least one of his fellow mortals about his need and the Savior who could meet it . . .

One day in Chicago Mr. Moody and I were riding up Randolph Street together in a streetcar right alongside of the city hall. The car could scarcely get through because of the enormous crowds waiting to get in and view the body of Mayor Carter Harrison, lying in state after his assassination. As the car tried to push its way through the crowd, Mr. Moody turned to me and said, "Torrey, what does this mean?" "Why," I said, "Carter Harrison's body lies there in the city hall and these crowds are waiting to see it." Then he said, "This will never do, to let these crowds get away from us without preaching to them; we must talk to them. You go and hire Hooley's Opera House (which was just opposite the city hall) for the whole day." I did so. The meetings began at nine o'clock in the morning, and we had one continuous service from that hour until six in the evening, to reach those crowds.

Mr. Moody was a man on fire for God. Not only was he always "on the job" himself, but he was always getting others to work as well. He once invited me down to Northfield to spend a month there with the schools, speaking first to one school and then crossing the river to the other. I was obliged to use the ferry a great deal; it was before the present bridge was built at that point. One day he said to me, "Torrey, did you know that that ferryman that ferries you across every day was unconverted?" He did not tell me to speak to him, but I knew what he meant. When some days later it was told him that the ferryman was saved, he was exceedingly happy.

Once, when walking down a certain street in Chicago, Mr. Moody stepped up to a man, a perfect stranger to him, and said, "Sir, are you a Christian?" "You, mind your own business," was the reply.

Mr. Moody replied, "This is my business."

The man said, "Well, then, you must be Moody."

Out in Chicago they used to call him in those early days "Crazy Moody," because day and night he was speaking to everybody he got a chance to speak to about being saved. One time he was going to Milwaukee, and in the seat that he had chosen sat a traveling man. Mr. Moody sat down beside him and immediately began to talk with him. "Where are you going?" Mr. Moody asked. When told the name of the town, he said, "We will soon be there; we'll have to get down to business at once. Are you saved?"

The man said that he was not, and Mr. Moody took out his Bible and there on the train showed him the way of salvation. Then he said, "Now, you must take Christ." The man did; he was converted right there on the train.

Most of you have heard, I presume, the story President Wilson used to tell about D. L. Moody. Former president Wilson said that he once went into a barbershop and took a chair next to the one in which D. L. Moody was sitting, though he did not know that Mr. Moody was there. He had not been in the chair very long before, as former president Wilson phrased it, he "knew there was a personality in the other chair," and began to listen to the conversation going on. He heard Mr. Moody tell the barber about the Way of Life, and former president Wilson said, "I have never forgotten that scene to this day." When Mr. Moody was gone, he asked the barber who he was, and he was told that it was D. L. Moody, and former president Wilson said, "It made an impression upon me I have not yet forgotten."

On one occasion in Chicago, Mr. Moody saw a little girl standing on the street with a pail in her hand. He went up to her and invited her to his Sunday school, telling her what a pleasant place it was. She promised to go the following Sunday, but she did not do so. Mr. Moody watched for her for weeks, and then one day he saw her on the street again, at some distance from him. He started toward her, but she saw him too and started to run away. Mr. Moody followed her. Down she went one street, Mr. Moody after her, up she went another street, Mr. Moody after her, through an alley, Mr. Moody still following, out on another street, Mr. Moody after her, then she dashed into a saloon and Mr. Moody dashed after her. She ran out the back door and up a flight of stairs, Mr. Moody still following; she dashed into a room, Mr. Moody following, and threw herself under the bed and Mr. Moody reached under the bed and pulled her out by the foot, and led her to Christ.

He found that her mother was a widow who had once seen better circumstances, but had gone down until now she was living over this saloon. She had several children. Mr. Moody led the mother and all the family to Christ. Several of the children became prominent members of the Moody Church until they moved away, and afterward became prominent in churches elsewhere. This particular child, whom he pulled from underneath the bed, was, when I was the pastor of the Moody Church, the wife of one of the most prominent officers in the church. Only two or three years ago, as I came out of a ticket office in Memphis, Tennessee, a fine-looking young man followed me. He said, "Are you not Dr. Torrey?" I said, "Yes." He said, "I am so-and-so." He was the son of this woman. He was then a traveling man, and an officer in the church where he lived.

When Mr. Moody pulled that little child out from under the bed by the foot, he was pulling a whole family into the kingdom of God, and eternity alone will reveal how many succeeding generations he was pulling into the kingdom of God.

D. L. Moody's consuming passion for souls was not for the souls of those who would be helpful to him in building up his work here or elsewhere; his love for souls knew no class limitations. He was no respecter of persons; it might be an earl or a duke or it might be an ignorant colored boy on the street; it was all the same to him; there was a soul to save and he did what lay in his power to save that soul.

A friend once told me that the first time he ever heard of Mr. Moody was when Mr. Reynolds of Peoria told him that he once found Mr. Moody sitting in one of the squatters' shanties that used to be in that part of the city toward the lake, which was then called, "The Sands," with a colored boy on his knee, a tallow candle in one hand and a Bible in the other, and Mr. Moody was spelling out the words (for at that time he could not read very well) of certain verses of Scripture, in an attempt to lead that boy to Christ.

Oh, young men and women and all Christian workers, if you and I were on fire for souls like that, how long would it be before we had a revival? Suppose that tonight the fire of God falls and fills our hearts, a burning fire that will send us out all over the country, and across the water to China, Japan, India, and Africa, to tell lost souls the way of salvation!

7. Endued with Power from on High

The seventh reason God used D. L. Moody was that *he had a very definite enduement with power from on high, a very clear and definite baptism with the Holy Ghost.* Mr. Moody knew he had "the baptism with the Holy Ghost," he had no doubt about it. In his early days he was a great hustler, he had a tremendous desire to do something, but he had no real power. He worked very largely in the energy of the flesh. But there were two humble Free Methodist women who used to come over to his meetings in the YMCA. One was "Auntie Cook" and the other Mrs. Snow. (I think her name was not Snow at that time.) These two women would come to Mr. Moody at the close of his meetings and say, "We are praying for you."

Finally, Mr. Moody became somewhat nettled and said to them one night, "Why are you praying for me? Why don't you pray for the unsaved?"

They replied, "We are praying that you may get the power." Mr. Moody did not know what that meant, but he got to thinking about it, and then went to these women and said, "I wish you would tell me what you mean," and they told him about the definite baptism with the Holy Ghost. Then he asked that he might pray with them and not they merely pray for him.

Auntie Cook once told me of the intense fervor with which Mr. Moody prayed on that occasion. She told me in words that I scarcely dare repeat, though I have never forgotten them. And he not only prayed with them, but he also prayed alone. Not long after, one day on his way to England, he was walking up Wall Street in New York (Mr. Moody very seldom told this and I almost hesitate to tell it), and in the midst of the bustle and hurry of that city, his prayer was answered; the power of God fell upon him as he walked up the street, and he had to hurry off to the house of a friend and ask that he might have a room by himself, and in that room he stayed alone for hours; and the Holy Ghost came upon him, filling his soul with great joy, so that at last he had to ask God to withhold His hand, lest he die on the spot from such joy.

He went out from that place with the power of the Holy Ghost upon him, and when he got to London (partly through the prayers of a bedridden saint in Mr. Lessey's church), the power of God wrought through him mightily in North London and hundreds were added to the churches. That was what led to his being invited over to the wonderful campaign that followed in later years.

Time and again Mr. Moody would come to me and say, "Torrey, I want you to preach on baptism with the Holy Ghost." I do not know how many times he asked me to speak on that subject. Once, when I had been invited to preach in the Fifth Avenue Presbyterian Church, New York (invited at Mr. Moody's suggestion; had it not been for his suggestion the invitation would never have been extended to me), just before I started for New York, Mr. Moody drove up to my house and said, "Torrey, they want you to preach at the Fifth Avenue Presbyterian Church in New York. It is a great, big church, cost a million dollars to build it." Then he continued, "Torrey, I just want to ask one thing of you. I want to tell you what to preach about. You will preach that sermon of yours on 'Ten Reasons Why I Believe the Bible to Be the Word of God' and your sermon on 'The Baptism with the Holy Ghost.'" Time and again, when a call came to me to go off to some church, he would come up to me and say, "Now, Torrey, be sure and preach on the baptism with the Holy Ghost." I do not know how many times he said that to me.

Once I asked him, "Mr. Moody, don't you think I have any sermons but those two: 'Ten Reasons Why I Believe the Bible to Be the Word of God' and 'The Baptism with the Holy Ghost'?" "Never mind that," he replied, "you give them those two sermons." . . .

I shall never forget the eighth of July 1894, to my dying day. It was the closing day of the Northfield Students' Conference—the gathering of the students from the eastern colleges. Mr. Moody had asked me to preach on Saturday night and Sunday morning on "The Baptism with the Holy Ghost." On Saturday night I had spoken about "The Baptism with the Holy Ghost, What It Is, What It Does, the Need of It and the Possibility of It." On Sunday morning I spoke on "The Baptism with the Holy Spirit, How to Get It." It was just exactly twelve o'clock when I finished my morning sermon, and I took out my watch and said, "Mr. Moody has invited us all to go up on the mountain at three o'clock this afternoon to pray for the power of the Holy Spirit. It is three hours to three o'clock. Some of you cannot wait three hours. You do not need to wait. Go to your rooms, go out into the woods, go to your tent, go anywhere where you can get alone with God, and have this matter out with Him."

At three o'clock we all gathered in front of Mr. Moody's mother's house (she was then still living) and then began to pass down the lane, through the gate, up on the mountainside. There were 456 of us in all; I know the number because Paul Moody counted us as we passed through the gate.

After a while Mr. Moody said, "I don't think we need to go any farther; let us sit down here." We sat down on stumps and logs and on the ground. Mr. Moody said, "Have any of you students anything to say?" I think about seventy-five of them arose, one after the other, and said, "Mr. Moody, I could not wait till three o'clock; I have been alone with God since the morning service, and I believe I have a right to say that I have been baptized with the Holy Spirit." When these testimonies were over, Mr. Moody said, "Young men,

I can't see any reason why we shouldn't kneel down here right now and ask God that the Holy Ghost may fall upon us just as definitely as He fell upon the apostles on the day of Pentecost. Let us pray." And we did pray, there on the mountainside. As we had gone up the mountainside, heavy clouds had been gathering, and just as we began to pray, those clouds broke and the raindrops began to fall through the overhanging pines. But there was another cloud that had been gathering over Northfield for ten days, a cloud big with the mercy and grace and power of God, and as we began to pray our prayers seemed to pierce that cloud and the Holy Ghost fell upon us. Men and women, that is what we all need—the baptism with the Holy Ghost.

13

The Personality of the Holy Spirit

AT THE PODIUM

Torrey's final years in ministry were marked by two things. First, he had an increasing focus on preaching Christian doctrine, so that his sermons seemed more and more to have the character of systematic theology instruction, or catechizing his congregation in fundamental truths. Second, he relentlessly emphasized what he called the baptism in the Holy Spirit. Torrey's view of the work of the Spirit occupies an unusual position in the history of evangelical ideas on the subject. Since the 1890s he had been preaching that believers should pray through and ask God for a definite baptism, or a first-time filling that empowered ministry supernaturally. But when Pentecostalism came on the scene around 1906, Torrey made it clear that he did not mean the same thing as that movement. He continued preaching his same message about what he called Spirit baptism well into the 1920s, even as Pentecostalism co-opted the language for its own experiences. Torrey's view aligns more nearly with a Keswick spirituality of empowerment, which is not quite what most noncharismatics teach but also not quite identical with Pentecostal or Charismatic teaching.

These two emphases of his later years—doctrinal comprehensiveness and an emphasis on a definite experience of the Holy Spirit for ministry—come together remarkably in this opening chapter from Torrey's most comprehensive book on the Holy Spirit. His keynote is the idea that the Holy Spirit is not a force but a person, and that failure to recognize this leads to all sorts of errors and defects in Christian experience.

Source: R. A. Torrey. *The Personality of the Holy Spirit: The Holy Spirit and What He Does and How to Know Him in All the Fulness of His Gracious and Glorious Ministry.* New York: Revell, 1927, 11–40.

We begin a series of [messages] on the person and work of the Holy Spirit by considering what the Bible has to say about the Holy Spirit as a person. It is impossible to rightly understand the work of the Holy Spirit, or to get into right relation with the Holy Spirit Himself—and thus know His blessed work in our own souls—without first coming to know the Holy Spirit as a person. One of the most fruitful sources of error and misconception, of unwholesome enthusiasm and false fire and fanaticism, in the treatment of this whole subject, is from trying to know the work of the Holy Spirit before we first come to know the Holy Spirit Himself. So my subject today is, "The Personality of the Holy Spirit."

To many of you this topic will seem like a rather abstract, abstruse, and impractical subject to take up with a popular audience. I do not blame you if you think so, for I can remember very distinctly the time when I so thought. The first popular address I ever heard upon the subject of the personality of the Holy Spirit was given by the late Dr. James H. Brooks, of St. Louis, that giant of Bible teaching. Of course I had heard lectures upon the subject in the theological seminary, but this was an address before a popular audience.

When Dr. Brooks had finished his address, I said to myself, "Well, Dr. Brooks has proved his point. The Holy Spirit certainly is a Person; but what difference does it make anyhow whether the Holy Spirit is a divine Person, or whether the Holy Spirit is a divine influence that God the Father, who doubtless is a person, sends into our hearts? It is divine anyhow."

But afterward I came to find out that it made all the difference in the world. I discovered from the study of the Word of God, and from my own experience and the experience of others, that the doctrine of the personality of the Holy Spirit is not only fundamental but vital and immeasurably practical. Anyone who does not know the Holy Spirit as a person has not attained unto complete and well-rounded Christian experience. Anyone who knows God the Father, and God the Son, and does not know God the Holy Spirit has not attained unto the Christian conception of God, nor to a fully Christian experience.

Why the Doctrine of the Personality of the Holy Spirit Is Important

There are three reasons the personality of the Holy Spirit is important to us. *First, it is of the highest importance from the standpoint of worship.* If the Holy Spirit is a person, and a divine Person—and He is—and if you or I do not know Him as such, and think of the Holy Spirit merely as an impersonal influence or power, then we are robbing a divine Person of the worship that is His due, of the love that is His due, and of the faith and confidence and surrender and obedience and worship that are His due.

May I ask each one of you, "Do you worship the Holy Spirit?" Theoretically we all do every time we sing the long meter Doxology:

Praise God from whom all blessings flow,
Praise Him all creatures here below,
Praise Him above, ye heavenly hosts,
Praise Father, Son, *and Holy Ghost.* [emphasis added]

Theoretically we all do every time we sing the Gloria Patri:

Glory be to the Father,
And to the Son,

And *to the Holy Ghost.*
As it was in the beginning,
Is now,
And ever shall be,
World without end. Amen. [emphasis added]

But it is one thing to do a thing theoretically, and it is quite another thing to actually do it. It is one thing to sing words; it is quite another thing to realize the meaning and the force of the words that you sing.

I had a very striking illustration of this some years ago. I was going to a Bible conference in New York. I had to pass a city four miles from the grounds where the conference was held. I had a relative living in that city, and on the way to the conference I stopped to call upon my relative, who went with me to the conference. This relative was a Christian, she was much older than I, and had been a Christian much longer than I, and a member of a Presbyterian church at that. Brought up on the Shorter Catechism, she was thoroughly orthodox. I spoke that morning at the conference on the personality of the Holy Spirit. When the address was over and we were waiting on the veranda of the hotel for the trolley to take us back to the city, my relative turned to me and said, "Archie, I never thought of *It* before as a person." Well, I had never thought of "*It*" as a person, but thank God I had come to know *Him* as a Person.

Second, *it is of the highest importance from a practical standpoint that we know the Holy Spirit as a Person.* If you think of the Holy Spirit, as so many even among Christian people do today, as a mere influence or power, then your thought will constantly be, "How can I get hold of the Holy Spirit and use it?" But if you think of Him in the biblical way, as a Person of divine majesty and glory, your thought will be, "How can the Holy Spirit get hold of me and use me?" Is there no difference between the thought of man, the worm, using God to thresh the mountain, or God using man, the worm, to thresh the mountain? The former conception is heathenish; it does not differ essentially from the African fetish worshipper who uses his god. The latter conception, the thought of God the Holy Spirit getting hold of us and using us, is lofty, Christian, sublime.

Furthermore, if you think of the Holy Spirit merely as an influence or power that you are to get hold of and use, your thought will necessarily be, "How can I get more of the Holy Spirit?" But if you think of Him in the biblical way, as a Person, your thought will be, "How can the Holy Spirit get more of me?"

The former conception of the Holy Spirit as a mere influence or power that we are to get hold of and use leads inevitably to self-confidence, self-exaltation, and a parade of self. If you think of the Holy Spirit as an influence or power that you are to get hold of and use, and then fancy that you have received the Holy Spirit, the inevitable result will be that you will strut around as if you belonged to a superior order of Christians.

How much we see of that sort of thing. I remember a woman who once came to me at the Northfield Bible Conference at the close of an address and she said to me, "Brother Torrey, I want to ask you a question, but before I do, I want you to understand that *I am a Holy Ghost woman*." My, it made me shudder; it sent a chill over me. But if we think of the Holy Spirit in the biblical way, as a divine Person of infinite majesty, who comes to dwell in our hearts and take possession of us and uses as He wills, not as we will, it leads to self-renunciation, self-abnegation, self-humiliation. I know of no thought that is more calculated to put one in the dust and keep one in the dust than this great biblical truth of the Holy Spirit as a divine Person coming to take up His dwelling in our hearts, and to take possession of our lives and to use us as He in His infinite wisdom sees fit.

Third, *the doctrine of the personality of the Holy Spirit is of the highest importance from the standpoint of experience*. Thousands and tens of thousands of Christian men and women can testify to an entire transformation of their experience and of their service through coming to know the Holy Spirit as a Person. This address upon the personality of the Holy Spirit, which I have given in almost every city in which I have ever held a series of meetings, is in some respects seemingly upon the most abstruse and technical subject that I ever attempt to handle before a popular audience. Yet more men and women have come to me at the close of this address, and more have written to me afterward concerning it, testifying of personal blessing received, than of any other address that God has ever permitted me to give.

Four Proofs of the Personality of the Holy Spirit: 1. Distinctive Marks of Personality

Today let's look at three separate and distinct lines of proof of the personality of the Holy Spirit.

The first line of proof of the personality of the Holy Spirit is that *all the distinctive marks or characteristics of personality are ascribed to the Holy Spirit in the Bible.* What are the distinctive marks or characteristics of personality? *Knowledge, will, and feeling.* Any being who knows and wills and feels is a person. Often when you say that the Holy Spirit is a Person, people understand you to mean that the Holy Spirit has hands, and feet, and fingers, and toes, and eyes, and ears, and nose, and mouth, and so on. No, not at all. These are not the marks of *personality*; these are the marks of *corporeity.* The marks of personality are knowledge, will, and feels, and any being who knows, thinks, feels, and wills is a person whether he has a body or not. You and I, if our earthly life ends before the Lord's return, will cease to have bodies for the time being; we will be "absent from the body, and to be present with the Lord" (2 Corinthians 5:8), but we shall not cease to be persons; we will be persons still, even though we have no body.

Now, all three of these marks of personality are ascribed to the Holy Spirit in the Bible.

Turn in your Bibles to 1 Corinthians 2:11 to read about the first mark: "For what man knoweth the things of a man, save the spirit of man which is in him? even so the things of God knoweth no man, but the Spirit of God." *Here knowledge is ascribed to the Holy Spirit.* The Holy Spirit, in other words, is not a mere illumination that comes to your mind and mine, whereby our minds are enlightened and strengthened to see truth that they would not otherwise discover. No, the Holy Spirit is a Person who Himself knows the things of God and reveals to us what He Himself knows.

Now turn to 1 Corinthians 12:11 (RV): "But all these worketh the one and the same Spirit, dividing to each one severally even as he will." *Here a will is ascribed to the Holy Spirit.* The thought is that the Holy Spirit is a divine Person who gets hold of us and uses us according to His will. This is one of the most fundamental truths in regard to the Holy Spirit, and we must ever bear it in mind if we are to come into right relations with Him and continue in right relations with Him. Countless earnest-minded Christians are going astray at this point. They are trying to get hold of some divine power that they can use according to their will. I thank God from the depth of my heart that there is no divine power that I can get hold of to use according to my will. What could I do in my foolishness and ignorance with a divine power? What evil I might work! But while I thank God that there is no divine power that I can get hold of and use in my foolishness and ignorance according to my will, I am still more glad that there is a divine Person who can get hold of me and use me according to His infinitely wise and loving will.

Now turn to Romans 8:27, "And he that searcheth the hearts knoweth what is the mind of the Spirit, because he maketh intercession for the saints according to the will of God." What I wish you to note here is the expression, "the *mind* of the Spirit." The Greek word here translated "mind" is *phronema,* a comprehensive word that has in it all three ideas of knowledge, feeling, and will. It is the same word used in the seventh verse of this chapter, where we read, "The mind of the flesh is enmity against God" (RV), where the thought is that not merely the thought of the flesh is enmity against God, but the whole moral and intellectual life of the flesh is enmity against God.

We now turn to a most remarkable passage, Romans 15:30. "Now I beseech you, brethren, for the Lord Jesus Christ's sake, and for the love of the Spirit, that ye strive together with me in your prayers to God for me." What I wish you to notice particularly in this verse are these five words, "The love of the Spirit." It is a wonderful thought. It teaches that the Holy Spirit is not a mere blind influence or power, no matter how beneficent, that comes into our hearts and lives, but that He Himself is a divine Person, loving us with the tenderest love. *Here feeling, or emotion, is ascribed to the Holy Spirit.*

I wonder how many of us have ever thought much regarding "the love of the Spirit"? I wonder how many of us ministers who are here today have ever preached a sermon on "The Love of the Spirit." I wonder how many of you have ever heard a sermon on "The Love of the Spirit." I wonder how many of you have ever thanked the Holy Spirit for His love.

Every day of your life you kneel down before God the Father, at least I hope you do, and say, "Heavenly Father, I thank Thee for Thy great love that led Thee to give Thy Son Jesus Christ to come down into this sinful world and to die upon the cross of Calvary in my place." Every day of your life you kneel down and look up into the face of Jesus Christ the Son and say, "Thou blessed Son of God, I thank Thee for that great love of Thine that led Thee to come down to this world in obedience to the Father and to die in my place upon the cross of Calvary."

But do you ever kneel down and look up to the Holy Spirit and say to Him, "Holy Spirit, I thank Thee for Thy great love to me"? And yet we owe our salvation as truly to the love of the Spirit as we do to the love of the Father and the love of the Son. If it had not been for the love of God the Father to me, looking down upon me in my lost estate—yes, anticipating my fall and ruin and sending His own Son down to this world to die upon the cross in my place—I would have been a lost man today. If it had not been for the love of Jesus Christ the Son coming down to this world in obedience to the Father, and laying down His life, a perfect atoning sacrifice on the cross of Calvary in my behalf, I would have been a lost man today. But if it had not been for the love of the Holy Spirit to me, leading Him to come down to this world in obedience to the Father and the Son, to seek me out in my lost condition, following me day after day, and week after week, and month after month, and year after year, following me when I would not listen to Him, when I deliberately turned my back upon Him, when I insulted Him, . . . until at last He succeeded in bringing me to my senses and bringing me to realize my utterly lost condition, and revealing the Lord Jesus to me as just the Savior whom I needed and induced and enabled me to receive the Lord Jesus as my Savior and Lord—if it had not been for this patient, never-wearying love of the Spirit of God to me, I would have been a lost man today."

For another element of the Spirit's personality, let's turn to a passage in the Old Testament, Nehemiah 9:20, "Thou gavest also thy good Spirit to *instruct them*, and withheldest not thy manna from their mouth, and gavest them water for their thirst." *Here both intelligence and goodness are ascribed to the Holy Spirit.* I have brought this passage in merely because it is from the Old Testament. There are those who say that the doctrine of the personality of the Holy Spirit is in the New Testament but not in the Old Testament; but here we find it as clearly in the Old Testament. Of course, we do not find it as frequently in the Old Testament as in the New, for this is the dispensation of the Holy Spirit, but the doctrine of the personality of the Holy Spirit is there in the Old Testament.

There are many who say that the doctrine of the Trinity is not in the Old Testament. But the doctrine of the Trinity is in the Old

Testament in the very first chapter of the Bible. In Genesis 1:26 we read, "And God said, *Let us* make man in our image, after *our likeness*" (emphasis added). Here the plurality of the Persons in the Godhead stands out clearly. God did not say, "I will," or, "Let *me*" "make man in my own image." No, He said, "*Let us* make man in *our* image, after *our likeness*." The three persons in the Trinity are found in the first three verses in the Bible, "In the beginning God created the heaven and the earth"; here we have God the Father. "And the earth was without form, and void; and darkness was upon the face of the deep. And *the Spirit* of God moved upon the face of the waters"; there you have the Holy Spirit. "And God said," there you have the Word, "Let there be light: and there was light." Here we have the three persons of the Trinity in the first three verses of the Bible.

In actual fact the doctrine of the Trinity is found hundreds of times in the Old Testament. In the Hebrew Bible it occurs in most of the places where you find the word "God" in your English Bible, for the Hebrew word ordinarily used for God in the Old Testament is a plural noun; literally translated it would be "Gods," and not "God." In the very passage to which the Unitarians and Jews, who reject the deity of Christ, refer so often as proving conclusively that the deity of Christ cannot be true, namely, Deuteronomy 6:4, the very doctrine that they are seeking to disprove is found; for the verse, literally translated, would read, "Hear, O Israel: Jehovah our Gods is one Jehovah."

Why did the Hebrews, with their unquestionable and intense monotheism, use a plural name for God? This was the question that puzzled the Hebrew grammarians and lexicographers of the past, and the best explanation that they could arrive at was that the plural for God here used was the "*pluralis majestatis*," that is, the plural of majesty. But this explanation is entirely inadequate. To say nothing of the fact that the pluralis majestatis in the Old Testament is a figure of very doubtful occurrence—I have not been able to find any place in the Old Testament where it is clear that the pluralis majestatis is used—but in addition to that, even if it were true that the pluralis majestatis does occur in the Old Testament, there is another explanation for the use of a plural name for God that is far nearer at hand and far more adequate and satisfactory, and that is, that *the Hebrew inspired writers used a plural name for God, in spite of their intense monotheism, because there is a plurality of Persons in the one Godhead.*

For one more feeling of the Spirit, which shows His personality, let's turn to Ephesians 4:30: "And grieve not the holy Spirit of God, whereby ye are sealed unto the day of redemption." *Here grief is ascribed to the Holy Spirit.* In other words, the Holy Spirit is not a mere blind, impersonal influence or power that comes to dwell in your heart and mine. No, He is a Person, a Person who loves us, a Person who is holy and intensely sensitive against sin, a Person who recoils from sin in what we would call its slightest forms as the holiest woman on earth never recoiled from sin in its grossest and most repulsive forms. And He sees whatever we do, He hears whatever we say, He sees our every thought. Not a vagrant fancy is allowed a moment's lodging in our mind but what He sees it; and if there is anything impure, unholy, immodest, uncharitable, untrue, false, censorious, bitter, or unChristlike in any way, in word or thought or act, He is grieved beyond expression.

This is a wonderful thought, and it is to me the mightiest incentive that I know to a careful walk, a walk that will please this indwelling Holy One in every act and word and thought.

How many a young man is kept back from doing things that he would otherwise do, by the thought that if he did do that, his mother might hear of it and she would be grieved beyond expression. How many a young man who went over to France in the late war and was surrounded by the awful temptations that encompassed our young men on every hand at that time and at that place, in some hour of fierce temptation stood at the door of a house that no self-respecting man ought ever to enter, and just as his hand was on the doorknob and he was about to open the door, the thought came to him, "If I should enter there mother might hear of it, and if she did it would nearly kill her," and he has turned away without entering.

But listen, there is One holier than the holiest mother that you or I ever knew, One who loves us with a more tender love than our own mother loves us, and He sees everything we do, not only in the daylight but under the cover of the night; He hears every word we utter, every careless word that escapes our lips; He sees every thought we entertain, yes, every fleeting fancy that we allow a moment's lodging in our mind. If there is anything unholy, impure, immodest, uncharitable, indecorous, unkind, harsh, bitter, censorious, or unChristlike in any way, in act or word or thought, He sees it and is grieved beyond expression. Oh, how often there has come into my mind some thought or imagination, from what source I do not know, but a thought I ought not to entertain, and just as I was about to give it lodgment, the thought has come, "The Holy Spirit sees that and will be grieved by it," and the thought has gone.

Bearing this thought of the Holy Spirit in our mind will help us to solve all the questions that perplex the young believer in our day. For example, the question, "Ought I as a Christian to go to the theater or the movies?" Well, if you go, the Holy Spirit will go, too, for He dwells in the heart of every believer and goes wherever the believer goes. Were you ever in a theater in your life where you honestly thought the atmosphere of the place would be congenial to the *Holy* Spirit? If not, do not go. Ought I as a Christian go to dances? Well, here again, if you go, the Holy Spirit will surely go. Shall I as a Christian play cards? Were you ever at a card party in your life, even the most select little neighborhood gathering, or even at a home gathering to play cards, where you thought the atmosphere of the place would be congenial to the *Holy* Spirit? If not, do not play. So with all the questions that come up and that some of us find so hard to settle, this thought of the Holy Spirit will help you to settle them all, and to settle them right (if you really desire to settle them right and not merely to do the thing that pleases yourself, even though it may grieve the Holy Spirit).

2. Actions Only a Person Can Perform

The second line of proof of the personality of the Holy Spirit is that, *Many actions are ascribed to the Holy Spirit that only a person can perform*. There are many illustrations of this in the Bible, but I will limit our consideration today to three instances.

First, 1 Corinthians 2:10 declares, "But God hath revealed them unto us by his Spirit: for the Spirit searcheth all things, yea, the deep things of God." Here the Holy Spirit is represented as searching the deep things of God. In other words, as we have already said under our previous heading, the Holy Spirit is not a mere illumination whereby our minds are illumined and made strong to apprehend truth that they would not otherwise discover, but the Holy Spirit is a Person who Himself searches into the deep things of God, and He reveals to us the things that He discovers. Such words, of course, could only be spoken of a person.

Second, the apostle Paul writes, "Likewise the Spirit also helpeth our infirmities: for we know not what we should pray for as we ought: but the Spirit itself maketh intercession for us with groanings which cannot be uttered. (Romans 8:26). Here the Holy Spirit is represented as doing what only a person can do, that is, He is represented as praying. The Holy Spirit is not merely an influence that comes upon us and impels us to pray, nor is He a mere guidance to us in offering our prayers. No, no; *He is Himself a Person who prays.*

Every believer in Christ has two divine Persons praying for him every day: first, the Son, our "Advocate with the Father," who "ever liveth to make intercession for us" at the right hand of God in the glory (1 John 2:1 and Hebrews 7:25); second, the Holy Spirit who prays through us down here on earth. Oh, what a wonderful thought, that each and every believer in Christ has two divine Persons praying for him every day. What a sense it gives us of our security—I do not believe the Devil will ever get us.

When I started around the world in 1901, I sent out 5,000 letters to people whom I had learned knew how to pray, asking them if they would pray for Mr. Alexander and me every day as we went around the world. One of the hardest tasks I ever had in my life was signing those letters, signing my name 5,000 times, but it paid, for soon letters came back by the thousands from these persons saying that they would pray for us every day. When Mr. Alexander and I reached Melbourne, Australia, 10,000 people had taken it up and were praying for us every day, and when we reached England no less than 40,000 people were praying for us every day. Who could not preach under such circumstances, and is it any wonder that the marvelous results followed that did follow?

I wish they were all praying for me still. Yet, while I would be glad to have those 40,000 people praying for me every day, if I had to choose between having 40,000 of the godliest men and women on earth praying for me every day, or to have those two Persons, Christ the Son, our Advocate with the Father, and the Holy Spirit, our Comforter, praying for me every day, I would choose the two rather than the 40,000.

Third, consider these two closely related passages:

> But the Comforter, which is the Holy [Spirit], whom the Father will send in my name, he shall teach you all things, and bring all things to your remembrance, whatsoever I have said unto you." (John 14:26)

> I have yet many things to say unto you, but ye cannot bear them now. Howbeit when he, the Spirit of truth, is come, he will guide you into all the truth: for he shall not speak of himself; but whatsoever he shall hear, that shall

> he speak: and he will shew you things to come. He shall glorify me: for he shall receive of mine, and shall shew it unto you." (John 16:12–14)

In John 14:26 the Holy Spirit is represented as doing what only a person could do, namely, teaching. In the John 16 passage the Holy Spirit acts as a living, personal teacher. It is our privilege today to have the Holy Spirit, a living Person, as our teacher.

Every time we study our Bible it is possible for us to have this divine Person, the author of the Book, to interpret it to us, and to teach us its real and its innermost meaning. It is a precious thought. How many of us have often thought when we heard some great human teacher whom God has especially blessed to us, "Oh, if I could only hear that man every day, then I might make some progress in my Christian life." But listen, we can have a teacher more competent by far than the greatest human teacher that ever spoke on earth for our teacher every day, and that peerless teacher is the Holy Spirit.

3. The Office Can Only Be Based on a Person

The third line of proof of the personality of the Holy Spirit is that *an office predicated on the Holy Spirit could only be predicated on a Person*. Look, for example, at John 14:16–17: "And I will pray the Father, and he shall give you another Comforter, that he may abide with you for ever; even the Spirit of truth; whom the world cannot receive, because it seeth him not, neither knoweth him: but ye know him; for he dwelleth with you, and shall be in you." Here the Holy Spirit is represented as *another Comforter* who is coming to take the place of our Lord Jesus. Up to this time our Lord Jesus had been the friend always at hand to help them in every emergency that arose. But now He was going, and their hearts were filled with consternation, and He tells them that while He is going *another is coming* to take His place. Can you for a moment imagine our Lord

Jesus saying this if the other who is coming to take His place were a mere impersonal influence or power?

Can you imagine our Lord Jesus saying what He says in John 16:7—"Nevertheless I tell you the truth; It is expedient for you that I go away: for if I go not away, the Comforter will not come unto you; but if I depart, I will send him unto you"—if that which was coming to take His place were not another Person but a mere influence or power? In that case, is it for a moment conceivable that our Lord could say that it was expedient for Him, a divine Person, to go and a mere influence or power, no matter how divine, come to take His place? *No! No!* What our Lord said was that He, one divine Person, was going, but that *another Person, just as divine as He, was coming to take His place.*

This promise is one of the most precious promises in the whole Word of God for this present dispensation, the thought that during the absence of our Lord, until that glad day when He shall come back again; another Person just as divine as He, just as loving and tender and strong to help, is by my side always; yes, and He dwells in my heart every moment to commune with me and to help me in every emergency that can possibly arise.

I take it for granted that you know that the Greek word translated "Comforter" in these verses means far more than Comforter. The Greek word so translated is *Parakletos.* This word is a compound word, compounded of the words "*para,*" which means "alongside," and "*kletos,*" which means "one called": so the whole word means, "One called to stand alongside another," one called to take his part and help him in every emergency that arises.

It is the same word that is translated "advocate" in 1 John 2:1, "If any man sin, we have an advocate [*parakleton*] with the Father, Jesus Christ the righteous." But the word "advocate" does not begin to give the full force of the word. Etymologically the word "advocate" means about the same as the word "Parakletos." "Advocate" is really a Latin word transliterated into the English; the word is compounded of two words, "*ad*," meaning "to," and *vocatus*, which means "one called"; that is to say, "advocate" means one called to another to take his part, or to help him. But in our English usage, this word has obtained a narrower and more restricted sense. The Greek word, as I have already said, means, "One called alongside another," and the thought is of a helper always at hand with His counsel and His strength and any form of help that is needed.

Up to this time the Lord Jesus Himself had been the disciples' Paraclete, the friend always at hand to help. Whenever they got into any trouble, they simply turned to Him. For example, on one occasion they were perplexed on the subject of prayer and they said to the Lord, "Lord, teach us to pray," and He taught them to pray. On another occasion Jesus was coming to them, walking on the water. When their first fear was over and He had said, "It is I, be not afraid," then Peter said unto Him, "Lord, if it be thou, bid me come unto thee upon the water." And the Lord said, "Come." Then Peter clambered over the side of the fishing boat and commenced to go to Jesus, walking on the water.

He got along fine for a few moments, and then seemingly he turned around to see if his companions saw how well he was doing, thus he took his eyes off the Lord and saw the wind and the waves, and no sooner had he gotten his eyes off the Lord than he began to sink, and he cried out, "Lord, save me," and Jesus reached out His hand and held him up. Just so, when they got into any other emergency, the disciples tuned to the Lord and He delivered them.

But now He was going and consternation filled their hearts, and the Lord said to comfort them, "Yes, I am going, but another just as divine as I, just as loving and tender as I, just as able to help in every emergency that may arise, is coming to take My place." This other Paraclete is with us wherever we go, every hour of the day or night. He is always at our side. Precious and wondrous thought!

4. Always at Our Side

If this thought gets into your heart and stays there, you will never have another moment of fear as long as you live. How can we fear under any circumstances if we really believe that He is by our side? You may be surrounded by a howling mob. I have been, an Irish mob and a Chinese mob, but what of it, if He walks between you and the mob? That thought will banish all fear.

Some years ago I was speaking at a Bible conference at a lake in New York. A cousin had a cottage four miles up the lake, and I went up there and spent my rest day with him. The next day he brought me down in his steam launch to the pier where the conference was held. As I stepped off the launch onto the pier, he said to me, "Come back again tonight, Archie, and spend the night with us," and I promised him I would. But I did not realize what I was promising.

That night, when my address was over, as I went out of the hotel and started on my walk, I found that this was a large undertaking. The cottage was only four miles away, which was nothing to me under ordinary circumstances, but a storm was coming up and the whole heaven was overcast. Furthermore, the path led along a bluff bordering the lake, and the path was near the edge of the bluff. Sometimes the lake was perhaps not more than ten or twelve feet below, at other times some thirty or forty feet below. I had never gone over the path before and found that it led right along the edge of the bluff. Besides that, there was no starlight and I could not see the path at all. There had already been a storm that had gulleyed out deep ditches across the path into which one might fall and break his leg. I could not see these ditches except when there would be a sudden flash of lightning, when I would see one, and then it would be darker and I blinder than ever.

As I walked along this path, so near the edge of the bluff with all the furrows cut through it, I felt it was perilous to take the walk and thought of going back; but the thought came to me, "You promised that you would come tonight and they may be sitting up waiting for you," so I felt that I must go on. But it seemed creepy and uncanny to walk along the edge of the bluff on such an uncertain path, which I could not see, while rising from the foot of the bluff were the sounds of the wailing and the moaning of the lake as it was moved by the fast approaching storm.

Just then the thought came to me, "What was it you told the people there at the conference about the Holy Spirit being a Person always by our side? Does He not walk by your side now?" Then I at once realized that the Holy Spirit walked between me and the edge of the bluff, and that four miles through the dark was four miles without fear, a gladsome instead of a fearsome walk.

I once threw this thought out in the Royal Albert Hall in London, one dark dismal afternoon. A young lady in the audience had an abnormal fear of the dark. It simply seemed impossible for her to go into a dark room alone. After the meeting was over, she hurried home and rushed into the room where her mother was sitting and cried, "Oh, Mother, I have heard the most wonderful address this afternoon I ever heard in my life, about the Holy Spirit always being by our side as our ever-present helper and protector. Mother, I shall never be afraid of the dark again."

But her mother was a practical English woman and said to her, "Well, let us see how real that is. Now, go upstairs to the top floor, into the dark room, and shut the door and stay in there alone in the dark."

The daughter wrote me the next day, "I went bounding up the stairs, went into the dark room, closed the door, and it was pitch-dark, and oh, it was dark, utterly dark, but that room was bright and glorious with the presence of the Holy Spirit."

This thought of the Holy Spirit being a personal friend, ever present for us, is also . . . *a cure for all loneliness*. If the thought of the Holy Spirit as an ever-present friend, always at hand, enters your heart and stays there, you will never have another lonely moment as long as you live.

My life for the larger part of the last twenty-five years has been a lonely life. I have often been separated from my family for months at a time, sometimes I have not seen my wife for two or three months at a time, and for eighteen months I did not even once see any member of my family except my wife. One night I was walking the deck of a steamer in the South Seas between New Zealand and Tasmania. It was a stormy night. Most of the other passengers were below, seasick, and none of the officers or sailors could walk with me, for they had their hands full looking after the boat. Four of the five members of my family were on the other side of the globe, 17,000 miles away by the nearest route that I could get to them, and the one member of my family who was nearer was not with me that night.

As I walked the deck all alone, I got to thinking of my four children so far away and was about to get lonesome when the thought came to me of the Holy Spirit by my side, and that as I walked up and down the deck in the night and in the storm, He took every step with me, and all my loneliness was gone.

I gave expression to this thought some years ago in the City of St. Paul, and at the close of the address a physician said to me, "I wish to thank you for that thought. I am often called at night to go out alone through darkness and storm far into the country, and I have been very lonely, but I will never be lonely again, for I will know that every step of the way the Holy Spirit is beside me in my doctor's gig."

In this same precious truth of the Holy Spirit as a personal friend always at hand, there is a cure for a broken heart. Oh, how many brokenhearted people there are in the world today. Many of us have lost loved ones, but we need not have a moment's heartache if we only know "*the communion* of the Holy Ghost" (2 Corinthians 13:14). There is perhaps here today some woman who a year ago, or it may be only a few months or a few weeks ago, or possibly a few days ago, had by her side a man whom she dearly loved, a man so strong and wise that she was freed from all sense of responsibility and care, for all the burdens were upon him. How bright and happy were the days of his companionship! But the dark day came when that loved one was taken away, and how lonely and empty and barren and full of burden and care life is today. Listen, woman, there is One who walks right by your side today, who is far wiser and stronger and more loving and more able to guide and help than the wisest and strongest and most loving husband that ever lived. He is ready to bear all the burdens and responsibility of life for you, yes, ready to do far more, ready to come in and dwell in your heart and fill every nook and corner of your empty and aching heart, and thus banish the loneliness and all the heartache forever.

I said this one afternoon in St. Andrew's Hall in Glasgow. At the close of the address, when I went out into the reception room, a lady who had hurried out to meet me approached. She wore a widow's bonnet, her face bore the marks of deep sorrow, but now there was a happy look in her face. She hurried to me and said, "Dr. Torrey, this is the first anniversary of my dear husband's death (her husband was one of the most highly esteemed Christians in Glasgow), and I came to St. Andrew's Hall today, saying to myself, 'Dr. Torrey will have something to say that will help me.' Oh," she continued, "you have said just the right word. I will never be lonesome again, never have a heartache again. I will let the Holy Spirit come in and fill every aching corner of my heart."

Eighteen months passed, I was back in Scotland again, taking a short vacation on the Lochs of the Clyde, on the private yacht of a friend. One day we stopped off a point, a little boat put off the point and came alongside the steam yacht. The first one who clambered up the side of the yacht and over the rail and onto the deck was this widow. Seeing me standing on the deck, she hurried across and took my hand in both of hers, and with a radiant smile on her face, she said, "Oh, Dr. Torrey, the thought you gave me in St. Andrew's Hall that afternoon stays with me still, and I have not had a lonely or sad hour from that day to this."

The Power to Preach: The Spirit Beside Me

But it is in our Christian work that the thought comes to us with greatest power and helpfulness. Take my own experience: I became a minister of the Gospel simply because I had to, or be forever lost. I do not mean that I am saved by preaching the Gospel; I am saved simply on the ground of the atoning blood of Jesus Christ, and that alone; but my becoming a Christian and accepting Him as my Savior turned upon my preaching the Gospel. For several years I refused to come out as a Christian because I was unwilling to preach, and I felt that if I became a Christian, I must preach. The night that I surrendered to God, I did not say, "I will accept Christ," or "I will give up my sins"; I said, "I will preach."

But if there was ever a man who by natural temperament was utterly unfitted to preach, it was I. I was an abnormally bashful boy, and a stranger could scarcely speak to me without my blushing to the roots of my hair. When I went away from home visiting with other members of my family, I could not eat enough at the table, I was so frightened to be among strangers. Of all the tortures I endured at school, there was none so great as that of reciting a piece. To stand on the platform and have the scholars looking at me, I could scarcely endure it; and even when my own father and mother at home asked me to recite the piece to them before I went to school, I simply could not recite it before my own father and mother.

Think of a man like that going into the ministry. Even after I was a student in Yale College, when I would go home on a vacation and my mother would have callers and send for me to come in and meet them, I could not say a word. After they were gone my mother would say to me, "Archie, why didn't you say something to Mrs. S— or Mrs. D—?" and I would say, "Why, Mother, I did." And she would reply, "You did not utter a sound." I thought I did, but it would get no farther than my throat and stick there.

I was so bashful that I never even spoke in a church prayer meeting until after I entered the theological seminary. Then I thought that if I were to be a preacher, I must at least be able to speak in my own church prayer meeting. I made up my mind that I would. I learned a piece by heart, I remember some of it to this day, but I think I forgot some of it when I got up to speak that night.

As soon as the meeting was open, I grasped the back of the settee in front of me and pulled myself up to my feet and held on to it lest I should fall. One Niagara went rushing up one side and another down the other, and I tremblingly repeated as much of my little piece as I could remember, and then dropped back into the seat. At the close of the meeting a dear old maiden lady, a lovely Christian woman, came to me and said, "Oh, Mr. Torrey, I want to thank you for what you said tonight. It did me so much good, you spoke with so much feeling." Feeling? The only feeling I had was that I was scared nearly to death. Think of a man like that going into the ministry.

My first years in the ministry were torture. I preached three times a day. I committed my sermons to memory, and then I stood up and twisted the top button of my coat until I had twisted the sermon out, and then when the third sermon was preached and finished, I dropped back into the haircloth settee back of the pulpit with a great sense of relief that that was over for another week. But then the dreadful thought would at once take possession of me, "Well, you have got to begin tomorrow morning to get ready for next Sunday." Oh, what a torment life was.

But a glad day came, a day when the thought that I am trying to teach you now took possession of me, namely, that when I stood up to preach, that, though people saw me, that there was Another whom they did not see but who stood by my side, and that all the responsibility was upon Him and all I had to do was to get just as far back out of sight as possible and let Him do the preaching. From that day to this, preaching has been the joy of my life; I'd rather preach than eat. Sometimes when I rise to preach, before I have uttered a word, the thought of Him standing beside me, able and willing to take charge of the whole meeting and do whatever needs to be done, has so filled my heart with exultant joy that I can scarcely refrain from shouting.

Just so in your Sunday school teaching. Some of you worry about your Sunday school class for fear you will say something you ought not to say, or leave unsaid something you ought to say, and the thought of the burden and responsibility almost crushes you. Listen! Always remember this, as you sit there teaching your class: There is One right beside you who knows just what ought to be said and just what ought to be done. Instead of carrying the responsibility of the class, let Him do it, let Him do the teaching.

One Monday morning I met one of the most faithful laymen I ever knew, and a very gifted Bible teacher. This Monday morning as I called upon him at his store, he was greatly cast down over the failure in his class, or what he regarded as failure. He unburdened his heart to me, and I listened. Then when he had finished I said to him, "Mr. Dyer, did you not ask God to give you wisdom as you went before that class?" He said, "I did."

Then I said, "Did you not expect Him to give it?"

"I did."

"What right have you to doubt that He did?"

"I never thought of that before," he answered. "I will never worry about my class again."

Just so in your personal work. When I or someone else urges you at the close of the meeting to go and speak to someone else, oh, how often you want to go, but you do not stir. You think to yourself, "I might say the wrong thing. I might do more harm than good." Well, you will say the wrong thing if you say it. Yes, if you say it, you certainly will say the wrong thing, but trust the Holy Spirit to do the talking and He will say the right thing through you. Let Him have your lips to speak through. It may not appear to be the right thing at the time, but sometime you will find that it was just the right thing.

One night in Launceston, Tasmania, as Mrs. Torrey and I went away from the meeting, my wife said to me, "Archie, I wasted the whole evening. I have been talking to the most frivolous girl you ever saw. I don't think she had a serious thought in her head, and I spent the whole evening with her."

"Clara, how do you know that you wasted the evening? Did you not ask God to guide you?"

"Yes."

"Did you not expect Him to?"

"Yes."

"Well, leave it with Him."

The very next night at the close of the meeting, the same seemingly utterly frivolous young woman came up to Mrs. Torrey, leading her mother by the hand, and said, "Mrs. Torrey, won't you speak to my mother? You led me to Christ last night, now please lead my mother to Christ."

But I must close. There is another line of proof of the personality of the Holy Spirit, but we have no time to dwell upon it.

To sum it all up: The Holy Spirit is a Person. Theoretically, we probably all believed that before, but do you in your real thought of Him, in your practical attitude toward Him, treat Him as a Person? Do you really regard the Holy Spirit as just as real a Person as Jesus Christ—just as loving, just as wise, just as tender, just as strong, just as faithful, just as worthy of your confidence and your love, and surrender as He? Do you think of Him as a divine Person always at your side? The Holy Spirit was sent by the Father into this world to be to the disciples of our Lord in this present dispensation, after our Lord's departure and until His return, to be to you and me, just what Jesus Christ had been to His disciples during the days of His personal companionship with them on earth. Is He that to you? Do you know "*the communion* of the Holy Spirit," the companionship of the Holy Spirit, the partnership of the Holy Spirit, the fellowship of the Holy Spirit, the comradeship of the Holy Spirit? To put it all into a single word, I say it reverently, the whole object of this address is to introduce you to my friend, the Holy Spirit.

APPENDIX

Torrey's Autobiography

Entitled simply "Autobiography," this undated manuscript by R. A. Torrey is held in Moody Bible Institute's archives as part of the Moodyana collection. It has never been published; it is edited to conform to contemporary spelling and style.

I first faced the question of accepting Christ as my Savior when I was thirteen years of age. I was in a large room on the third story of our home in Geneva, New York, where we put the old books out of the library. It was a favorite pleasure of mine to go up there and rummage through some of these old books. One day I picked up the Covenant of the First Presbyterian Church of Geneva, New York, of which my mother was a member, and thought to myself that I wondered if I could not be a church member. I began to read and assented to everything I read till I came to something to the effect that if I became a Christian, I must be ready to go wherever God told me to go and to do whatever God told me to do and to be whatever God told me to be.

I then closed the pamphlet and threw it away, saying to myself,

"Just as likely as not, God would tell me to be a preacher and I have determined to be a lawyer," which profession a great many of our family had already followed; and I decided then and there I would not be a Christian, and I went in for a life of pleasure. I was very worldly, but time and time again the thought that I must preach came before me. On one occasion I was sleeping in a certain room in our house in Geneva, and I dreamed that my mother was dead, though in point of fact at the time, she was sleeping (or possibly she was praying) in another room across the broad hall. I dreamed that my mother came floating in at the window where I was actually sleeping, as an angel and very beautiful (she was a beautiful woman, anyway), and came and stood by my bedside and begged me to be a preacher and I promised her that I would. I started from my sleep and found it to be a dream, but I could not get away from it; it haunted me for years.

One day in my junior year (I think it was) in college, Professor Northrup, professor of rhetoric (afterward president of the University of Minnesota), in showing us how to line an essay or an address, took the subject "A Call to the Ministry." Everything he said made me uneasy, though I tried to persuade myself that I had no call to the ministry. Later in my junior year, while leading a very reckless life, drinking very heavily (though I was only seventeen years of age, or possibly it was late in the year and I may have been eighteen), I awoke one night in awful agony and despair.

In desperation I sprang out of bed, rushed to my washstand drawer, and drew it open to take out of it the instrument that would put an end to the whole business by committing suicide; but I could not find it and in the dark I dropped on my knees beside the open drawer and promised God that if He would take the awful burden off my heart, I would preach the gospel. I did not say that I would accept Christ, nor that I would become a Christian but that I would preach. I settled it then and there that I would preach but I did not accept Christ; in fact, I did not know what it meant to accept Christ. I made no change whatever in my life; in fact, I think my life, if anything, was wilder after that than it was before, but I did tell people that I intended to be a preacher, but I think everybody considered that I was joking, for I certainly lived in no such way as one who expected to be a minister of the Gospel should live.

Later on in my college course (in my senior year) I read "*Ecce Homo*": that made a great impression on me, as did also J. G. Holland's *Bay Path* and Nathaniel Hawthorne's *Scarlet Letter*. *Ecce Homo* especially made it clear to me (though it is not by any means an orthodox book) that I ought to come out and make a public confession of Christ. As I had been known in college as anything but a Christian, I felt that I ought to make my public confession of Christ then and there, and so did in the college chapel and united with the college church.

The best I knew I tried to live a Christian life, making a radical change in my conduct, but I was received into the church in a very careless way. There was no pastor of the college church at that time. I met President Porter one day as I went to one of his lectures on psychology, and I said, "President Porter, I wish to unite with the church." He replied, "Are you clear about that?" I replied, "I am." "Well," he said, "you are a clear-minded man." And that was all the examination that I had before being received into the church.

I entered Yale Theological Seminary the following autumn. I had read my Bible every day of my life without a single exception since I was thirteen years of age, and I had read it a good deal before that, for we were all trained at home to read the Bible every day. I had prayed every day of my life, even through my most worldly days. I was trained to pray so early that I cannot remember when it was done; doubtless it was done by my mother but I have no recollection of it, though I can remember back till when I was three years old. It was undoubtedly before I was three that I was taught the habit of daily prayer.

While in the seminary I read a great deal of all sorts of literature, and, among others, agnostic literature. I had not been interested enough in Christianity to be an agnostic before but took it for granted that Christianity was true, and was not interested enough to inquire. Through the influence of this reading (especially through the reading of Gibbon), I became utterly unsettled in my faith, and doubted whether the Bible was the Word of God, whether Jesus Christ was the Son of God, and whether there was any God. I was utterly at sea. I was not an atheist but an agnostic, not an infidel but a skeptic. I suppose there were those in seminary to whom I could have gone and who could have helped me, but I did not go to any, except to one other student who did not help me at all.

I made up my mind to find out to an absolute certainty the truth. I decided that if the Bible was the Word of God, I would find that out and act accordingly, and if it was not, I would find that out and act accordingly. I determined I would find out whether there was a personal God, and that if I could find out there was, I would act accordingly and if I found out there was not, I would act accordingly; and I found out—not in a day or a month or a year—but I found out to an absolute certainty that there was a God, that Jesus Christ was the Son of God in a sense that no other being was the Son of God, a divine Person. I found out to an absolute certainty that the Bible was the inerrant Word of God.

In my seminary days, even after I was saved from agnosticism, I was very liberal; in fact, I think I may say that I was the leader of the new theology and destructive criticism wing in the seminary while I was there. The professors in Yale Seminary at that time were all orthodox (according to present-day test they would have been called extremely orthodox), but I was not. I read a great deal of Unitarian literature and got a great deal of help from it, because Unitarianism was more advanced toward the truth in its thinking than I was at that time. My graduating thesis was on transcendentalism. I was a great admirer of Theodore Parker, Channing, and others of the same or similar schools.

European Trip, Circumstances, Schools, and Teachers

I gave up my first pastorate, in Garrettsville, Ohio, in 1882. I had a great desire for further study and determined to go to Germany, to study especially dogmatic theology and Christian evidences. I was in the University of Leipzig and Erlangen in 1882 and 1883. I was already married and Mrs. Torrey accompanied me. At Leipzig I studied under Granz Delizsch and Professors Luhardt and Kahnis. Dr. Delizsch was, at that time, the leading authority in Hebrew and Old Testament criticism in Germany. I not only studied under him in the classroom but also in private gatherings to the few American students. I gave more time to Professor Luhardt than to Professor Kahnis. Luhardt was perhaps the leading authority in doctrinal theology and apologetics at that time in the Lutheran Church in Germany. Kahnis was the great authority in church history.

When I left Leipzig I went to call on Professor Delizsch to bid him goodbye. He received me with great kindness and affection; he asked me where I was going, and I told him to Erlangen (he had formerly been a professor there); he said, "Well, you need letters of introduction," and gave me letters of instruction to Professor Frank, the pronounced thinker and the leading Hegelian in Germany at that time, and also a letter to the most prominent liturgist in Germany at that time, who was also a professor in the University of Erlangen. Frank was the rector of the university. Then as I left, Professor Delizsch took me by the hand wand walked down the hall with tears in his eyes as he bid me goodbye.

When I reached Erlangen, where I went in 1883, I found that these letters of introduction meant far more than I had dreamed. The professors to whom they were directed not only received me graciously in their classrooms but called upon myself and wife at our home, and Professor Frank especially made intimate friends of us. I had already read before going to Erlangen Frank's two great books. He said to me on one occasion, "Mr. Torrey, do not merely come into my classes but come to my house and let me personally direct your studies, and you study in my library and the university library under my personal direction." Of course, I accepted this kind offer, and it meant far more to me than the work in the classroom. Professor and Mrs. Frank showed both Mrs. Torrey and myself very many kindnesses, and we kept up our acquaintance with them as family friends for many years after we had returned to America. At Erlangen I studied not only under Frank but also under Professor Zahn, one of the great authorities in his one line.

Minneapolis and Church Ministries

After my return I organized the Open Door Church in late 1883 or in the beginning of 1884. I led that church three years, and then became superintendent of the City Missionary Society, from 1886 to1889, when I organized the People's Church in the heart of the city. For three years I preached or taught six nights every week. Sunday services were held largely in theaters and places of public resort. On Sundays I would go down to my church (three miles from my home) in the morning and have continuous services either in the hall or else in the open air, oftentimes having nine or ten services a day in the summer time, and not returning to my home until perhaps eleven or twelve o'clock at night.

Here are the churches where I served as pastor: (1) Congregational Church, Garrettsville, Ohio; (2) the Open Door Church, Minneapolis, Minnesota; (3) People's Church, Minneapolis, Minnesota; (4) Chicago Avenue Church (later named the Moody Church), Chicago; and (5) The Church of the Open Door, Los Angeles.

Teaching Weekly Union Sunday School Lessons

Probably in 1886 I began teaching the Union Sunday School Lessons in Minneapolis, meeting in a public hall Saturday afternoon, with teachers and other Christians from all over the city (perhaps four or five hundred) in weekly attendance. The classes were originally intended to be taught one month by one minister and the next month by another. The first month was given to Rev. Dr. David Burrell, at the present time pastor of the Marble Collegiate Church in New York. The second month was given to me, and I had the class from that time until I left Minneapolis in 1889. Later I taught the Union Sunday School Lessons in Chicago, meetings being held first in the auditorium of the YMCA for several years. Still later the lessons were transferred to the Moody Church, which was of much larger capacity, where every Saturday night I taught the lesson to 2,000 or more people, until leaving to go around the world.

The Call to the Chicago Bible Institute

In the summer of 1889 I received a letter from Rev. John Collins, who had been a classmate of mine both in college and seminary, and also had been secretary of the International Christian Workers' Association (of which I was president through its entire history), asking me if I had heard from D. L. Moody, and saying that he had had a long talk with Moody and that Moody was intending to give me a big swing in Chicago. I had, however, not heard from D. L. Moody. Later I met Rev. E. M. Williams, pastor of the Congregational Church in Northfield, Minnesota (I had held evangelistic meetings in his church and with Carlton College). In meeting me, he said, "Have your ears burned this summer?" I said, "No." "Well," he said, "I should think they would, for I have been talking about you a great deal to Mr. D. L. Moody." I afterward learned that he had told Mr. Moody something about my work and also about my meetings with him. I think it was his suggestion that led Mr. Moody to invite me to Chicago. I think that F. H. Revell also had something to do with it. I had presided at the First International Christian Workers' Convention in Chicago, and Mr. Revell and others were so impressed with the way the meetings were conducted and the smoothness with which they proceeded that they told Mr. Moody, and Mr. Moody had said to some one of them, "A man that can control a group of people like that is a man I want."

When Mr. Moody organized his preliminary conferences in the spring of 1889 (looking forward to the organization of the Bible Institute), I had a great desire to go, but I was unable to get to the conferences. Then I heard of Mr. Moody's proposed conference in September 1889 and wished to go to that, and I received a letter from Mr. Moody inviting me to the conference. I wrote him that I was a very busy man but that if he had anything specific, he wanted me to do, I should be glad to go, but otherwise I did not see how I could leave my work. To that letter I got no reply, though I afterward learned that he had replied to it.

When the time for the conference came, I made up my mind that I would go anyhow, but up till within two or three hours of starting for Chicago I did not have the money to pay my fare but felt confident it would come. I got the money shortly before leaving, hurried home and told my wife that I was going. When I reached Chicago I found out that I had mistaken the date and was a day too early. I called on Mr. Ensign, superintendent of the Sunday School Union, and with whom I had some slight acquaintance. Almost the first thing he said to me was, "Have you seen Mr. Moody?" I replied that I had not. "Well," he said, "he wants to see you. He is over at 228 La Salle Avenue."

I went over to the office. I had not seen Mr. Moody for years, and though I had worked six weeks in his inquiry meeting in New Haven, naturally he had forgotten me, but as I entered his office, Mr. Merton Smith, who knew me, introduced me to him. Mr. Moody at once arose and said, "Oh, I want to have a talk with you," took me down to the rear of 228 La Salle Avenue, laid before me all his plans for the Institute, and said, "I want you to take this." I replied, "I have a work in Minneapolis that I do not know how I can leave." He said, "I do not want you to answer without praying over it. When you decide let me know."

I prayed over it for several days. I could not see how I could leave Minneapolis, and yet I had a great longing to go to Chicago. On the Sunday of the week when the conference was to close, it became perfectly clear to me that I ought to accept Mr. Moody's invitation, and on Friday, before the evening session, I told Mr. Moody I had decided. He asked me what my decision was. I replied, "I am coming." He replied, "Get home just as quickly as you can, and get back as quickly as you can. I will need you more next week than I do now." He asked me when I would be back, and I replied, "Tuesday morning, at nine o'clock."

I took the train that night for Chicago and reached there Saturday morning, told my wife that we were going to Chicago and I wanted all the furniture on the train by Monday night at six o'clock. We got professional packers and the furniture was all on the train, marked for Chicago; Mrs. Torrey and the children did not come till later, in order that I might have a home settled for them there. At exactly nine o'clock, I walked into the LaSalle Avenue entrance to the church and lecture room. Dr. Weidner was giving a lecture to the new Institute. As I entered from the street, Mr. Moody stepped into the hall from Dr. Weidner's lecture, where he had introduced him.

Mr. Moody looked at me with a start and said, "Where did you come from?" I replied, "Minneapolis." He said, "How did you get here so soon?" I replied, "What time did I tell you I would be here?" He replied, "You said you would be here at nine o'clock Tuesday morning." I said, "Look at your watch," and it was exactly nine o'clock. I had Mr. Moody's confidence from that time on.

Acknowledgments

I would like to thank the Torrey Honors Institute of Biola University for giving me the extra time needed to publish this book. My thanks also to the students of the Torrey Honors Institute who have read and discussed these sermons with me and with each other over the past five years. And a special thank-you to Roger Overton for his work preparing the manuscript.